To Kahts —
you were always
in my corner, and I
appreciate you!
Meow !.!.

KAY "KRO" KROGER

Book Design by: *Simon Jay Cervania*

PREFACE

~ A Note on Wheels ~

A prayer wheel is a meditation device that spins; inside the prayer wheel are scrolls of the sutras. As it spins, the sutras spin too. Each rotation is a recitation of the sutra. Each revolution is a single step on the lifetimes-long journey towards transcendence. And each turning of the wheel represents a turning of the Wheel of Dharma, and the Eightfold Path of the Buddha's teachings.

I was meditating one day, when I had this thought: The Wheel of Dharma interlocks with the Wheel of the Year. They joined like two cogs in a clock. For a moment I felt the seasons turning in their endless round; I saw equinoxes rolling past solstices; I saw lifetimes rolling past lifetimes in the spiral of

reincarnation.

The Earth spins on its axis. A dawn follows each night, and a dusk follows each day. The moon spins around the Earth, waxing and waning into fullness and emptiness. The tides endlessly reach up and pull back. The Earth moves around the sun. In Chicago (where I was born) and northern Europe (where many of my ancestors were born), the seasons turn in four quarters that follow the death and rebirth of the sun.

Everything in our solar system circles around the sun. Our solar system circles the galactic center once every two hundred and fifty million years.

In this great spiral, the souls of all beings spin as well. This collection represents my own place in the great turning. Each poem is a prayer, an act of devotion, a cry into the night, and an attempt to locate myself in the cosmos.

Some of the prayers are for things that are very small; some of them are for things that are very big. These seasons have, at times, been cause for great celebration and joy. At other times there has been stillness, uncertainty, and fear. One follows the other, as day follows night and winter follows autumn.

As a Buddhist and a practitioner of druidry, I feel these turnings deeply. As a bard, I write about them. This book is a circle and a spiral. You can start wherever you are, and you won't end up where you started. You'll wind up deeper and further inwards.

These writings are my personal research and understandings. I have arrived at these conclusions over the course of my life. I am not infallible, and some of the connections I draw may not resonate with you. I honor my own journey of learning as well as yours. Take what resonates with you, and leave what doesn't.

May your feet find the path easily and always.

May your legs carry you far and fleet. May your belly never know hunger, and your throat never know thirst. May your hands hold things of great beauty, and your arms always be strong enough help those in need. May your tongue say kind words, and may your eyes behold wonders. And may the spirit of Imbas light a fire in your head.

Many blessings,

TABLE OF

chapter title

featured artist

insight

poems

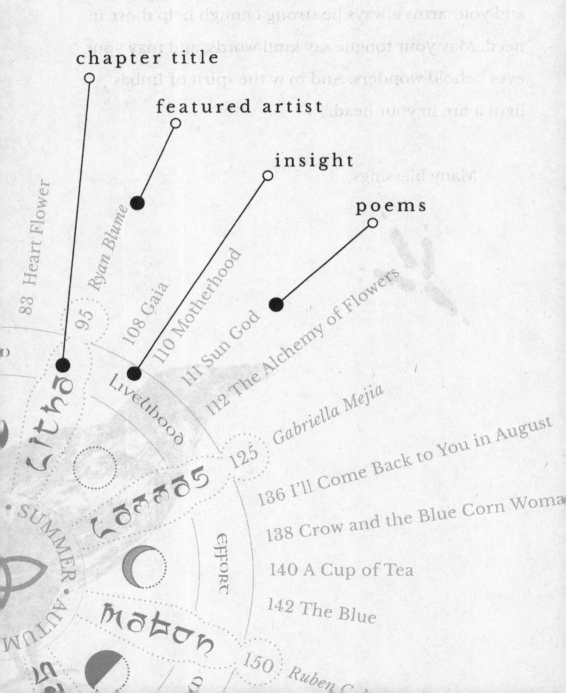

CONTENTS

> > *This book is based on the cycles of the pagan Wheel of the Year, and Buddhist Wheel of Dharma, which is the reason why the table of contents has a circular design. Please note the featured elements of each chapter.*

Each chapter includes the following:

An excerpt from the Heart Sutra

Featured Art

Meaning of the Title / Festival

Lesson in the cycle of Day

Lesson in the cycle of Year

Lesson in the cycle of Life

Insight of the Eightfold path

Poems reflecting each path / holiday

InterACTivity: *activities to help you understand each lesson*

Meditation practice

CONCENTRATIO

GRATITUDE

AUTUMN · MABON

LEAVES

EFFORT

Livelihood

Mindfulness

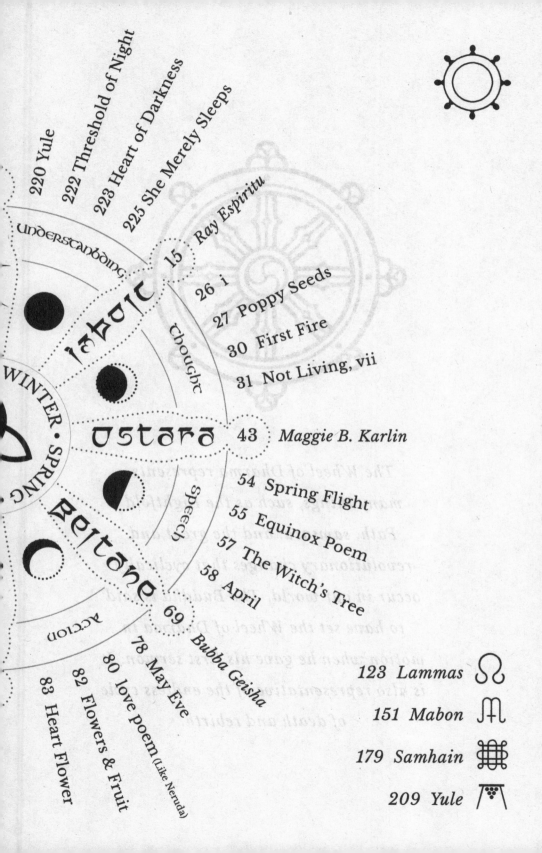

*The Wheel of Dharma represents
many things, such as the Eightfold
Path, samsara, and the great and
revolutionary changes that cyclically
occur in our world. The Buddha is said
to have set the Wheel of Dharma in
motion when he gave his first sermon. It
is also representative of the endless cycle
of death and rebirth.*

The Wheel of the Year represents the cyclical changes that occur throughout the fourfold cycle of seasons experienced in the Northern Hemisphere: winter, spring, summer, and fall. It stands for the birth and death of all things, and, in many ways, the larger and smaller cycles of our lives: the cycle of the day, the cycle of seasons, and even the cycle of the human lifetime.

oṃ namo bhagavatyai ārya prajñāpāramitāyai!

ārya-avalokiteśvaro bodhisattvo gambhīrāṃprajñāpāramitā caryāṃ
caramāṃo vyavalokayati sma:
panca-skandhās tāṃś ca svābhava śūnyān paśyati sma

from: the Heart Sutra

Imbolc

Imbolc is the quickening of life. The lambs are being born, their mother's milk is flowing, and the agricultural New Year has begun. The origin of the name is not definite, but may be linked to Old Irish i mbolg, or "in the belly" referring to the pregnancy of animals, especially sheep.

The Celtic New Year was marked by the death of the old year at Samhain. The rebirth of the sun at the solstice coincides roughly with the modern New Year (well, ten days earlier). Imbolc marks the beginning of the agricultural year, observed in Eastern countries as the Lunar New Year, which falls on the second new moon after the winter solstice. The sun's descent at Samhain, rebirth at Yule, and waxing at Imbolc marks a period of descent, rebirth, and renewal.

In the Day: Dreaming Forward

In the daily cycle, this phase of the year corresponds with deep sleep and dreams. This is the time of day before dawn when we are all curled up in our beds. Our unconscious minds are painting dreams at full steam. It shows us a jumbled, colorful spray of images that represent our deepest desires, private thoughts, and inner truths (and sometimes, utter nonsense). This is the time to dream forward: to think about what you wish to accomplish in the coming year.

You can bring these inner dreams into the world if your conscious mind is brave enough to admit what you want. It's time to sort through your metaphorical store of seeds. Those "seeds" are your secret hopes and desires; you need to decide which seeds (e.g. actions, goals, or outcomes) you wish to "plant" and "harvest" this year. What do you dream of? What do you seek to accomplish? What are the concealed, half-forgotten dreams of your childhood that you allowed yourself to abandon?

In the Year: The Goddess Brigid

Brigid is the patron of the fili, the vision-poets who practice aisling, or far-seeing and dream-vision. Considering her association with dreams, it is also appropriate to honor her during the holiday. Imbolc, also known as Brigid's Day, is often marked by the appearance of the Spring's first foliage such as snowdrops.

This is Brigid's holiday; she is the patron goddess of creative and skillful acts (especially blacksmithing), the lofty arts (such as law, philosophy, and poetry), healers, and the hearth. Imbolc is the time to honor Brigid and the waxing fire of the sun, and the sustaining fire of the hearth that has kept you warm through the winter. Though you may not have a physical hearth, she is also represented in humankind's mastery over the technologies of flame and heat that allow us to stay out of winter's frigid grasp.

At this time, the land seems to be giving birth, just like the cows and the sheep. The literal milk of livestock and the metaphorical milk of the Goddess

are flowing. The people have endured a long and difficult winter and a long and difficult journey within themselves. Now, the land begins to gift the people with new food to supplement the greatly-diminished winter stores.

Winter was a time of uncertainty and fear for the ancient Celts and all peoples who lived far from the equator. In places where the weather was severe, they were always carefully tallying how much food they had left. They worried about illness ravaging their communities. They wondered if mothers, the very young, or the very old were strong enough to make it through the bitter season. If there was an emergency and they needed outside help, winter weather could prove an impenetrable barrier to aid. No help was coming.

Though Brigid is associated with the fire of the hearth, she is also associated with the water of the springs, rivers, and lakes. This may seem counter-intuitive, as fire and water are often seen as opposing elements. In Celtic legend, visions from the spirit world or poetically-inspired dreams were often described as "fire burning upon the water." And Brigid is the goddess of seers and poets.

Both elements are necessary for the creation of the sword: in the heating of the forge and in the quenching of the blade—and remember, Brigid is the patron of blacksmithing. A helpful visualization may be that of the warmth of the mother's breast (fire) and the nourishment of her milk (the water). The ancient Celts ritually lighted fires and purified themselves with well water at this time.

In the Lifetime: Infants

In the cycle of the lifetime, Imbolc corresponds to (very) young childhood. If the rebirth of the sun at Yule is the birth, then Imbolc represents the babe suckling at the breast—calling back to the milk as it begins to flow from the sheep and cows, and by extension, the earth.

In modern Pagan cosmology, the North (Yule) corresponds with the element of Earth, and the East

(Ostara) corresponds with the element of Air. Imbolc falls between the two. This holiday is held between the airy mind and the earthly body. It is a time to dream with the mind what one might manifest into the physical world.

Babies are still dependent on their mother; their focus is on growing, exploring, and getting stronger. Everything is bright and new, and also a bit scary. They are still in an extreme yin, or passive, phase of life. They are wholly dependent on others. The receptive power of yin leaves their minds wide open to explore and to learn.

We could all learn from this mentality. At this time of year, try to embody this wide-eyed and open-minded curiosity. Allow everything to seem new, so that you can look at it without the pre-formed judgments and expectations you've developed throughout your life. We can only gain new perspectives when we shed old ones.. When we allow ourselves to become dreamers, it's easy to remember our dreams.

RIGHT INTENTION

When the sun is reborn at Yule, we are at the birth of Right Understanding. Imbolc aligns with Right Intention, the second principle of the Eightfold Path. At Right Understanding, we learn that everything is impermanent. (For more information, skip to the Right Understanding section.) Once we understand this, we can do something.

But what do you do with the knowledge that everything changes? That we can't hold onto anything forever? There are two paths. We can be cynical and angry: if nothing lasts, why should we care? Many nihilists have opted for this viewpoint.

Alternatively, we can ask: why would we waste any time being cruel to each other? Why would we squander our precious moments obsessing over material possessions or being power-hungry and unkind?

Right Intention is internal; we are still in the yin phase of winter. But we can begin to dream. How could we use this knowledge of impermanence out in the world? What kind of lifeway do we hope to build with this knowledge in our hearts? What intentions do you plant?

The Eightfold Path says that we should live a life where we cultivate loving-kindness for ourselves and for others. It asks us to cultivate self-knowledge through reflection. That way, we can understand when our intentions are motivated by anger or pettiness. It doesn't ask for us to miraculously wipe away the times when we get angry. It doesn't demand that we suddenly become angels of white light who are unable to feel negative emotions.

It is a pattern to practice. When we notice ourselves getting riled up, and about to lash out and hurt others, Right Intention says that we should remove ourselves from that situation briefly. Don't react—respond. Bring intentionality to your interactions; when we allow our nervous systems to get hijacked by intense emotions, we don't act with intention. So take time to cool your head; experience the emotion, and then let it pass. Intend to be better— and with diligence and time, you will be.

i

I am a nerve, single, raw
pressed against the sky
and the electric thunder of stars

perceiving all the vastnesses of time and pebbles
simultaneously; the whirl of color on cicada carapace
and the smears of supernova finger-painted across the
sky

everything hurts; there is too much of it
one set of hands cannot hold years, or moments
night folding forward into the sun

galaxies spin, refracted in cactus spines
hummingbirds drinking from thorny trees
a cosmos of pollen and dew

Poppy Seeds

The first thing I saw on New Years day
was a fox leaving footprints in the snow
on fire against a world so white
it looked like reality
forgot to wake up that day.

So I spread seeds in the winter
knowing they will sprout
sowing dreams in the stars
knowing they'll fall back down
in the white.
That's how poppies like to grow
germinated in the chest of February
stretching roots towards the equinox.

To bring visions to the bees
and color to the eye
that ephemeral light
is a glowing thing
with the descent of night
and the ascent of Spring.

So gather all your hopes up in bags
and stand at the train station
in the in-between of what was
and what could be.

There's a reason
we celebrate in the cold
and light candles
in the eyes of sleeping giants.

The world is stirring beneath its blanket,
feel it's pulse with
the dreamscape of it all.
Hold your hand against a naked tree
feel the leaves exploding inside it
you are no different.

You holy snowstorm
scatter the Earth with your poppy seeds
sacrifice all of those who would chain you
on the altar of your own self-worth.
Hold yourself to the same standard
to which the trees hold the sun.

Pick yourself up from these streets in your heart
because you are the sky
the blinking blue eye of God themself.
You are an alchemy of clouds
dreaming of new ways to give water to the world.
Give your water to the world.

Because when they thaw
they will remember the thirst
for everything they could have been
so for them
be everything you can be:
the poppy to the bee
each stowed dream
each sleeping, naked tree
and breathe
possibility.

First Fire

First flowing of life
milk-sweet
from the Earth
the sun's lengthening track
across the sky
traces the breast of the hills
dappled with snow.

In the Imbolg dawn,
Brigid lights a torch
stepping lightly on each hearth
spreading snowdrops on the ice.
Lambs are birthed
under the light of the oncoming dawn.

Not Living, vii

I spent all my Sundays giving birth to poems:
carving language around the growing stars,
cracked hearts and the flight of crows
venturing between letters and life.

Life's moon has waxed; I only visit, now:
good years easing gently towards the grave,
in the end. This is an old way of dying
warm, quiet, and alone.

Some mangle it into a way of living:
without wonder;
coffee that's getting cold,
a car payment, a tea kettle.

Ill-perceived suns wheeling;
a universe pulsing and grieving
while they scratch cats and forget:
reading poems instead of living in them.

This is a life that culminates in death

a flower blooming and rotting simultaneously.

Dying poorly is inexcusable.

One must write poems.

So, dream.

InterACTivity

In the cycle of the day, Imbolc sits before dawn, when we dream. The night sky is not only a field of stars, but a field of dreams. In the cycle of a lifetime, Imbolc sits at the time of infancy and childhood. What did you dream of becoming when you were young? Did you want to be an astronaut, a marine biologist, or a writer? Dig deep down into the hopes and aspirations you had before the world told you what you could and couldn't be. It doesn't matter how outlandish or how impossible they may seem now.

Take those dreams and draw them on the next page. You can be as literal or as abstract as you like.

If you're self-conscious about your technical skills, feel free to let your inner second grader draw for you. Once you've finished drawing your childhood dreams, take a step back. Look at the tapestry you've created. These are the secret hopes that lived at the center of your being; as you connect with your inner child, give yourself permission to believe in a world where anything is possible—like you used to.

Now take the images you've drawn on the page and imagine how you can apply them to your life as it stands today.

As a next step, create a vision board outside of the pages of this book.

Imagine how your life might look if you got back in touch with the dreams of your younger self. You are cultivating the fertile bed into which you will eventually plant the seeds of intention later this year.

Meditation: ʀɪɢʜʇ ɪɴʇɛɴʇɪᴏɴ

Buddhist teachings demand that we strive to understand the root of our actions. Even if an action has a beneficial end, if the intention behind it was harmful then there was still harm done inside you.

Right Intention is like the North Star—we must continually check that we are moving towards it. We must continually check that our intentions are based in compassion so that our lives will proceed in a direction of knowledge and growth.

Set aside some time in a quiet place where you won't be disturbed. Find a comfortable seat. Breathe in through your nose and out through your mouth. Do it a second time. And a third. Relax your body. Release any tension in your mind.

Think of something you currently desire in your life. Now, ask yourself: why do you want it? What are your underlying motivations? Sit with this question for as long as you need.

Keep in mind that multiple (and conflicting!) motivations can exist simultaneously. As you unearth your motivations, do not judge them, or yourself. Simply observe them. This exercise will help you understand your desires, and your motivations. As you move towards greater understanding of yourself, venture forth with compassion.

Imbolc, Right Intention

The triple aspect of the Buddha is known as the
Trikaya. This is a Mahayana Buddhist teaching
that speaks to both the nature of reality and
to the nature of Buddhahood. It states that the
Buddha has three aspects: the dharmakaya or
ultimate reality, the Sambhogakaya or divine
incarnation, and the nirmanakaya or physical
manifestation. Together these pieces represent
the infinite whole.

The Triple Goddess is represented by her three aspects of the Maiden, the Mother, and the Crone. The Maiden represents youth and innocence. The Mother represents adulthood and generative power. The Crone represents old age and the wisdom that comes with long life. These are represented by the three phases of the moon: waxing crescent, full, and waning crescent.

iha śāriputra: rūpaṃ śūnyatā śūnyataiva rūpaṃ; rūpān na pṛthak
śūnyatā śunyatāyā na pṛthag rūpaṃ; yad rūpaṃ sā śūnyatā; ya śūnyatā
tad rūpaṃ. evam eva vedanā saṃjñā saṃskāra vijñānaṃ.

iha śāriputra: sarva-dharmāḥ śūnyatā-lakṣaṃā, anutpannā aniruddhā,
amalā avimalā, anūnā aparipūrṃāḥ.

from: the Heart Sutra

Ostara

Ostara
Spring Equinox

The Spring Equinox, known as Eostre or Ostara, is located in the East of the Wheel. The East is also where the element of Air dwells in the modern Pagan cosmology. The word "east" derives from the Proto-Indo-European *aus- "to shine," or "dawn."

In the Day: dawn and hausos

There are numerous goddesses of the dawn (and by extension, the eastern direction) throughout the Indo-European world: Eostre (Celtic), Aurora (Roman), Eos (Greek), Ushas (Vedic), and more. They all trace their linguistic root back to Hausos, a Proto-Indo-European deity whose name derives from the word for East (*aus-).

Dawn is the time of beginnings and possibilities. We rise and decide how we will spend this cycle of the sun. What will we accomplish? How will we devote our time? How will we nourish our lives? Imbolc was the wee hours before the dawn when we dreamed; at dawn, we wake and put our dreams into action. We bring the dreams of our subconscious into the physical world. The spring equinox marks our emergence, our birth, from the dream of winter into the reality of the waking world.

In the Year: plαnτιng

As a deity of the dawn, Eostre (another name for Ostara) is also a deity of Spring. The Spring Equinox is when the light overtakes the darkness—and dawn is when day overtakes night. The light continues to wax until it reaches its full strength at the summer solstice (the noon of the year) on the longest day.

Those aforementioned goddesses represent the bounty and prosperity of the Earth and the Spring.

The trees are flowering. The world is green again. Fertility abounds. As such, symbols of fertility are naturally associated with this holiday—in the case of Eostre, rabbits, and eggs. The Christian holiday of Easter (from Eostre) is a fairly obvious overlay of the original Pagan spring festivals. It is a celebration of the return of life and light, and the cessation of winter.

It is also when farmers are deciding what they want to plant and harvest for the year. From a literal standpoint, now is a good time to map out your garden, plan your crops, and start your seedlings. From a metaphorical standpoint, now is a good time to think about what you would like to focus on this year. And keep in mind that you have limited resources, and only so much time—just as you have only so much space in your physical garden, and only so much time to tend it.

In your metaphorical garden, think of a few things you would like to "grow" this year: friendships, career, art, etc. What practical steps you would take to "grow" these aspects of your life? Lay out your metaphorical garden plots, and think about how you

are going to tend and nourish them.

Eostre is a time of establishing priorities, drawing up action plans, and committing to a course. This doesn't mean setting an inflexible plan that absolutely cannot be changed. Rather, it means establishing a limited set of areas you would like to blossom this year. It's about setting up habits and establishing routines that will help your chosen priorities flourish. And your goal doesn't have to be something concrete, like losing a hundred pounds or getting a promotion. It can be as simple as making time for your friends and building closer connections. At Eostre, anything is open to you, should you choose it.

In the Lifetime: youth

This phase of the Wheel of the Year is associated with childhood, the early morning of life. The time of possibility, when the innocence of youth has not been tempered or crushed by the weight of experience.

As the sun rises, we are filled with the light of possibility. We can do anything (but not everything.) This is the time for wide-eyed exploration of the world with the wide-eyed wonder that we had as children. Back then, we used our imaginations to build magical worlds, deciding to be astronauts and fairies and librarians in the span of a single week. It was the time for experimentation and raw, messy, unfiltered creative power.

Now, as adults, we can still use that same imaginative faculty to construct a magical world in our real life. We can decide what we are going to carry forward into the year. This is the time to explore and try things on. Eventually, you'll have to settle on a few seeds of change and plant them in the garden of your life for the year. But let yourself have a messy, creative phase as you do so. After all, from the chaotic and messy rain and mud of spring, the plants and crops are reborn.

RIGHT SPEECH

The third spoke on the Wheel of Dharma represents Right Speech. The first two steps on the Eightfold Path are purely internal—having to do with your view of the world, and examination of your motivation and reasoning. These also correspond to the time of the year that is still internal, yin, and winter. Right Speech is the first step on the Eightfold Path that moves into the external world, and it does so correspondingly with the dawn at Eostre.

Right Speech has to do with the way you use your voice in the world. It involves not speaking falsehoods, and not using the power of your voice to purposely and malevolently hurt others. It means holding yourself to a standard of kindness and compassion in your speech.

From the Vacca Sutra, translated by Thanissaro Bhikkhu: "Monks, a statement endowed with five factors is well-spoken, not ill-spoken...Which five?

"It is spoken at the right time. It is spoken in truth. It is spoken affectionately. It is spoken beneficially. It is spoken with a mind of goodwill."

Right Speech doesn't mean not saying difficult truths. It does not mean abstaining from difficult conversations. It does not mean staying silent while atrocities are committed.

First, is the time right? A husband may be cheating on his wife, and you may believe that she deserves to know. However, the middle of Thanksgiving dinner is usually the wrong time to express this truth.

Second, is it true? A kind lie may turn out to be crueler than a hard truth. Oftentimes we speak lies out of convenience or wanting to spare ourselves from emotionally taxing conversations. Do your best to not speak falsehoods. Lies and falsehoods are webs in which we become caught. They cloud the mind and distort reality. Plus, lies are hard to remember; keeping your story straight can get tiring.

And to condense the final three: why is the truth spoken? Examine your motivation for speaking. Is it

to express a concern to a friend, or to raise your voice in the face of injustice? Is it to lift up those who have been harmed, to help those who are vulnerable? These are beneficial to yourself and others. Or is your voice being raised in anger and rage, to hurt someone?

Doing harm to someone who has harmed someone may feel rewarding, but it does little to help the situation. But using your powers of speech and critical thinking to solve problems is a noble and worthy aspiration.

Spring Flight

My heart is a crow in flight
over a canyon brightening in the sun
shaking the frost of winter from its wings
and the rasp of January from its voice.

It circles forward, like a chariot wheel
like a cycle, like the sun
launching itself into the universal space
and into the absoluteness of beginning.

Equinox Poem

Balancing a world in each palm
in a yellow dawn
the story women sing out
how the world is made.

Light nestles into dark
boy bends around girl
in the heart of me
song chases story.

Day overtakes night
two birds racing on the track of the sky
sun-crow and moon-swan
run yin-yangs all through me.

The momentary equinox
when noon and moon
kiss in the dust of stars
stirs a peace deep within me.

Before the summer burns my feet
but after the winter chills my sleep

all secret parts of me
are given equal time.

The woman in the descent of wombs
lady of darkness
pulling sadness out of me like ropes
quickening growth.

The god in the rise of suns
lord of light
the stag of summer
piercing the earth with his spear.

Their unending movements
blurred together like hummingbird heartbeats;
I steal this moment, stillness
in equal measure
by the equal night.

Man and woman rest in me
lay their heads down in my chest
ceasing their endless pursuits for a breath
for the quiet of a single morning.

The Witch's Tree

The mirror cracks along the length of me
refracted girl, brilliant boy
each shining puzzle piece a prism
glaring out from where my heart should be

Human soul, caught in the light of a witch's tree
a thousand winking eyes wavering
moments of glass that can only catch
an ear, an eye, a finger, a thigh

Cacophony of color
brightness blinding, painting over
the canyons where the world rent me:
tectonic

My reflection skews in the belly of a spoon;
prismatic color lights my stained-glass skin.
I tie all my bottles to branches with strings,
secretly, equally, I am all of these things

April

As the land breathes in
The Cailleach breathes out
Old Hag of winter
walking with her crooked stick
to the Well of Renewal.

Jumping in, wrinkles wash from her face
like snow from a juniper branch
like rain from the roof
like fear from my heart.

These spirits of my ancestors
walk a long path
a circle about the world
a cycle of seasons
a spiral going inwards
no wheel crossing the same river.

A bright young hand
shines like April's dawn
and a new spring:

she strips the haggard robes of winter
and stands, naked
stark as a star
belly bared to the world.

InterACTivity

It is hard to decide what to plant in a given year. Excitable gardeners want to grow everything, just as we have many ideas we wish we could bring to fruition. In reality, we only have so much time and attention in a given year. Just as we have only so much space in our garden.

We have to decide what we will focus on; what seeds are you planting—and what metaphorical seeds are you cultivating for your year ahead? You can choose only a few. This page limits you to three.

Write your intentions in the seeds.

You will notice roots coming out from the seeds.

On these roots, write words that represent the physical actions you will take to nurture these seeds this year.

What actions will you take to accomplish your goals?

InterACTivity

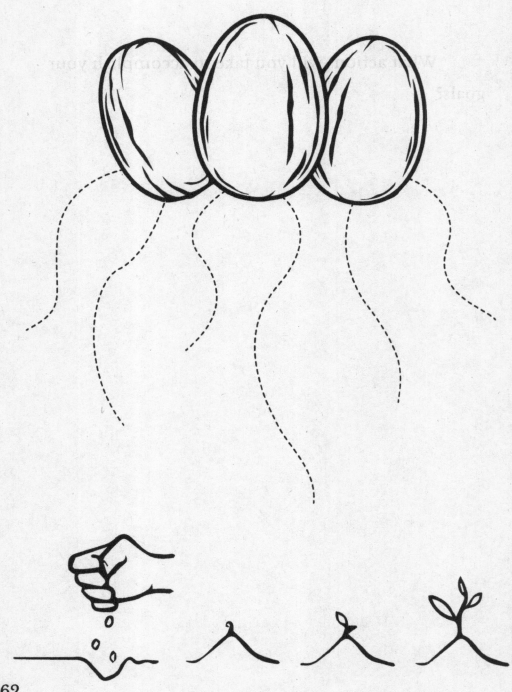

Ostara: Right Speech

Meditation: Right Speech

The East is the direction of the dawn and the element of air. Air lives in the human body in the lungs and in the throat, and we embody this element when we speak. In Buddhism, we embody Right Speech by cultivating communication that is rooted in discipline and Right Intention.

Find a quiet place where you won't be interrupted, and get comfortable. Take three deep breaths. Feel your body relax. Feel your thoughts begin to drift. Let them go, like clouds floating by in the sky. Take another three breaths. Sink into your breath, let yourself become nothing but your breath.

Now, think of a recent time when your words have had a powerful effect on someone—for good or for ill. What were the intentions behind your words? Did you use your words to help or hurt?

This is the season to actively consider how you use your powers of speech in the world. As you move through the Spring, think about how you can use your powers of speech to cultivate compassion and loving-kindness not only in yourself, but in your life.

ur motivations, do not judge them, or yourself.
Simply observe them. This exercise will help you
understand your desires, and your motivations. As
you move towards greater understanding of yourself,
venture forth with compassion.

The sacred tree of Buddhism is known as the Bodhi
Tree. Siddhartha Gautama sat beneath the Bodhi
Tree for 49 days without food or rest. At the end
of his meditation, he achieved enlightenment.
This tree is a tree of wisdom; it is the world
tree, its roots going down deep to the waters of
infinity, and its branches reaching up to the Void.
It is a place of refuge, where one is safe from the
tribulations and desires of this world.

The sacred tree in Paganism has many names, such as Yggdrasil. It is the axis mundi, or the connection between this and other worlds. It reaches up to the upper realms of the gods above, and the lower realms of the underworld below. It binds the cosmos together and is a bridge through which the consciousness can travel the worlds.

tasmāc chāriputra śūnyatayāṃ na rūpaṃ na vedanā na saṃjñā na samskārāḥ na vijñānam. na cakṣuḥ-śrotra-ghrāna-jihvā-kāya-manāṃsi. na rūpa-śabda-gandha-rasa-spraṣṭavaya-dharmāh. Na cakṣūr-dhātur. yāvan na manovijñāna-dhātuḥ. na-avidyā na-avidyā-kṣayo. yāvan na jarā-maraṃam na jarā-maraṃa-kṣayo. na duḥkha-samudaya-nirodha-margā. Na jñānam, na prāptir na-aprāptiḥ.

from: the Heart Sutra

BELTANE

Beltane

This word comes from Gaelic, specifically Lowland Scottish: bealltainn, which means "May first." It is a Celtic cultural and religious rite that marks the beginning of summer. A more ancient etymology may translate as literally "blazing fire," from Proto Indo-European (PIE) root *bhel- "to shine, flash, burn" added to the Old Irish ten "fire." Ten may also derive from PIE root *tep- "to be hot." This etymology is hotly debated, as fire was an important part of many Celtic holidays. It was, and is, a time of jumping over bonfires, and cattle were driven between two bonfires to inspire fertility and bounty in the coming year.

In the Day: ᗰIᗪᗰOᖇᑎIᑎG

The year turns past the equinox, and the days start to lengthen. The heat has started to build. The sun has crossed the horizon at sunrise, and begins to build towards High Noon. This morning time is when we have risen to action. We woke up, got out of our beds, had our breakfast, drank our coffee and tea, and stepped out the door and into the world. We may go to work, whether in an office or in the farm field. There is much to be done in the day, and an early start can help us accomplish what we plan. We've made our to-do lists; and we set out to complete them. This time of day signifies busy, deliberate action that is just starting to get into full swing.

In the Year: Alchemy

Alchemy is the art of transforming some dense, basic material into something lighter, brighter, and more valuable. We spent all winter dredging up our shadows and working with them. Beltane is the time to chuck them into the fire and transmute them into meaningful change. To adopt and embark on meaningful plans of action.

Beltane is the alchemical fire. It is transmutation. We are adding fuel to the fire, which will reach to its greatest height at the summer solstice. We spent all winter identifying the "lead." The "lead" is the harmful, negative, hurt, and damaged aspects of ourselves. The "gold" that we are calling forth from the lead is the new patterns of behavior. The "gold" is the new habits and thought patterns that will help us move through the world more gently and powerfully. It is the strengthened and more genuine relationships we forge. The time between Beltane and the summer solstice is the heat of the furnace into which we feed our lead. After that lead finishes cooking, it will return gold to us.

Each challenge, each shadow within us is a piece of lead. Looking at a challenge or trauma from a new perspective, and discovering how it can be a teacher, that is the alchemical process. Through this process, we are turning something heavy, which causes us sorrow, into something shining and valuable. When we do this, we make friends with the fire.

We often fear that fire will burn us. But when we approach it mindfully and with intention, we can work

73

together with fire to create beauty and mutual growth.

In the Lifetime: young Adulthood

We are in the midst of childhood at Eoster, and we reach young adulthood at Beltane. The fire will reach its greatest power at the summer solstice, just as we are at the height of our physical prime and ability in the noon of life, in maturity. Beltane is the late morning before we have come into our full strength, but when we begin to feel the stirrings of the fire.

The physical fire burns through us. Puberty roars through the body, stoking changes and growth— just as the sun stokes growth in the warming season, and the natural world comes to life. Sexual fire and energy are heavily associated with this holiday, appropriately—this is the time of life when sexual urges make themselves known to us, whatever form they take.

At this time of life, we are like the plants we cultivate at this time of year—vibrant and green, but spindly and ungainly. Without proper tending, it is unclear what form they will take. Without proper staking, a bean plant will fall over in a tangled mess. Without proper community support and channels of training, the brightening fire within us can lash out in unpredictable, harmful ways. We must carefully tend the waxing fire as we tend our growing sprouts, so that they may reach their full potential—without being drowned in too much water, or dried up in forgetfulness and neglect.

RIGHT ACTION

We moved from the internal world to the external world at Ostara; from the yin to the yang, from the night to the dawn, from the mind to the voice. We continue our journey outwards here by considering further how we move through the world, and how we interact with others.

Generally, Buddhism outright names a few things that shouldn't be done—killing, stealing, and sexual misconduct (which I choose to interpret as any form of sexual interaction that is not ethically conducted and/or that does not have the enthusiastic consent of all parties involved). Now, many don't hold these rules hard and fast. Raising animals and killing them compassionately falls within many's spectrum of "allowable" actions. And then there's the whole Starving Orphan on the Street Stealing Bread to Feed Their Sibling trope—which opens up more of a moral gray area.

Right Intention comes back into play here— for it's not only our actions that matter, but our motivations for our actions. It is the intention behind the action that must be accounted for, in addition to the action itself. Doing the right thing for a selfish reason may bring no harm into the world—but it will also bring no good or growth into your spirit. Consciously uncovering the motivations for your actions will help you know yourself and stoke the fires of compassion.

Action is movement; it is dynamic. It is fire. We must choose how we stoke our fires in the world. They can warm us in the winter and help us survive the darkness, or they can rage out of control and leave an ashy waste in their wake. How you cultivate your fire (actions) will majorly determine the kind of marks you leave on the world and in the hearts of those around you.

May Eve

Our copulation is among carnations
red flash on a flowered hillside
rendered shadow in the balefire flicker
tongue in the curve of your hip.

My love is a returning bird
an arrow against
the sky of you
migration of skin and season.

Always returning
to nest at your navel
a flash of indigo
against your belly:
the bluejay of me.

The branches around us
thicken with sap
arborvitae,
song swelling
your body, opening

radiance rising
pendulous, thriving.

And we roll
from the back of summer
stag-like, spent
on each other, on the world
carnations blooming in our hands.

love poem (Like Neruda)

she's in my mouth
bright and burning
ginger root.

she's singing in Spanish
the contents of a spice cart in her voice,
scattering paprika.

I love her
like Neruda loves:
with taste, and words, and poems.

I want her to waft through my heart
with the acridity of a tire fire,
small feet kicking sparks.

For her, I am ashes
an empty jar
inheriting wind and dried herbs:

Flammable, itchy
I want to be alight, on fire again
with things I cannot have.

Consumed in the cayenne smoke.

Flowers & Fruit

You and flower buds
swell with the summer.
Apple-blossoms cusping the promise
of harvest.

The smell of the blossoms of your belly
the sweet pollen of the navel and vulva:
the hibiscus hung
on rich, waxy leaves.

You are ripening, quickening
consummated,
pumping with the juice of life
and the heat of June.

You are a mango, a sun
sweeter fruit couldn't be hung
among jungle-coated continents;
reverent, I tend your gardens
of rising fire.

Heart Flower

I've always fallen in love too easily,
with the way sunlight sparkles on water,
a boy with seagull feathers in his hair,
with the shadow that nestles inside her hip bone,
mandolin music drifting from upstairs.

Magnolias blossom in all my gardens
coloring trees purple with painted pollen;
I wish they withered with the April rains
that they fell as the year turned forward
to decompose into loam and poems.

But my loves are weedy, persistent things
they root in a moment, and bloom for decades
eternally turning towards the sun,
building themselves from nothing
but dirt, air, and light.

If I were smarter, perhaps
I would wish for a soul of singularity, fidelity,

but those things make for such boring poetry.
How tragic for me, how fortunate for my art
that my spirit so easily ties itself up in knots.

What you are willing to sacrifice or "offer," in exchange for accomplishing your goal? What are you willing to give up so you can make room in your life? These new things will need that room.

Write what you are willing to give up on the empty page that follows. Then rip it out and set it aflame.

Burn it as an offering to the spirits. In keeping with the season, you may even consider jumping over the fire, visualizing yourself "jumping into action." Literally step into this new momentum towards your goals.

Please exercise proper forethought and take practical fire safety measures prior to conducting this activity. Do so outdoors with adequate ventilation. Perform this exercise at your own risk.

InterACTivity

What you are willing to sacrifice or "offer" in exchange for accomplishing your goal? What are you willing to give up so you can make room in your life? These new things will need that room.

Write what you are willing to give up on the empty page that follows. Then rip it out and set it aflame.

Burn it as an offering to the spirits. In keeping with the season, you my even consider jumping over the fire, visualizing yourself "jumping into action." Literally step into this new momentum towards your goals.

Please exercise proper forethought and take practical fire safety measures prior to conducting this activity. Do so outdoors with adequate ventilation. Perform this exercise at your own risk.

What am I willing to give up?

Meditation: Right Action

Most Buddhist schools advise five precepts: not killing, not stealing, not misusing sex, not lying, and not abusing intoxicants. Vietnamese Zen teacher Thich Nhat Hanh puts forward five trainings to aid oneself in the arena of Right Action. The five questions below reflect these trainings.

To consider these questions, seclude yourself somewhere without noise or distraction. Find a comfortable seat, and breathe deeply. Feel the tension going out of your body and mind. Breathe deeply again. Release your thoughts, and feel your mind clearing. In the stillness of your mind, consider Thich Nhat Hanh's questions:

Have you cultivated a respect for all life, and the desire to protect all living things?

Do you live in a way that is generous, without hoarding things you do not need?

Do you avoid sexual misconduct, entering into sexual encounters with ethics, openness, communication, and avoiding abuse?

Do you exercise loving communication and deep listening?

And finally, are you mindful of what you consume—not only food, but intoxicants, including media?

You can extend mindfulness in your life beyond these five questions.. We must live each moment fully present. We must be mindful of not only our actions, but the intentions behind those actions as well.

Traditional Chinese Medicine holds there to be three main energy centers (or Dan Tiens), which correspond to the gut, heart, and head. The Lower Dan Tien creates and stores jing, the energy of the physical body. The Middle Dan Tien creates and stores qi, the energy of our emotions and thoughts. The Upper Dan Tien creats and stores shen, the energy of spirit or consciousness.

The Celtic Druids likewise describe three energy centers in the body, described as the Three Cauldrons. They are the Coire Goiriath (Cauldron of Warmth), the Coire Ernmae (Cauldron of Vocation), and the Coire Sois (Cauldron of Knowledge). The Cauldron of Warmth is the wellspring of life within all of us. The Cauldron of Vocation is the connection between Self and the World. The Cauldron of Knowledge is the connection between Self and the Divine.

tasmāc chāriputra aprāptitvād bodhisattvasya prajñāpāramitām āśritya viharatyacittāvaraṇaḥ. cittāvaraṇa-nāstitvād atrastro viparyāsa-atikrānto niṣṭhā-nirvāṇa-prāptaḥ.

from: the Heart Sutra

Litha

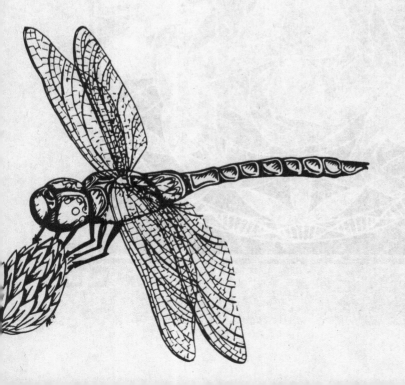

Litha

The Wheel of the Year has turned to Summer Solstice. Litha derives is name from Old Norse líða, which in turn evolved from Proto-Indo-European *leh₁tom, which meant "summer" or "warmth." The Northern Hemisphere has entered the season of the sun. The sun is visualized as a flaming wheel being pushed across the sky by a god or goddess—or pulled as a chariot wheel by heavenly steeds. It is the time in which we are at our greatest power, where we must put forth our greatest effort.

In the Day: NOON

The Solstice is the longest day of the year, when the sun is at its full power. Similarly, the sun is at the height of its power when it rides highest in the sky.

Aside from being the time of day when it is typically hottest, this is also the time of day that is the busiest. The work day is in full swing; the accelerating time of full morning has brought us to full speed at noon.

This is true not just for office jobs, but also for those who worked in traditional agricultural role as well in northern latitudes. Whether you're making calls or pitching hay bales, you've been working up a sweat for quite a few hours now. This is the time of day when you're moving ahead full force, crossing things off your list and attending to the needs of your life.

However, this is also the time of day when most people sit down for a break and a meal. Just as momentum is important, so is remembering to nourish yourself. You can't pour from an empty glass; keeping your tank full is important to keep you going. And that's not just your stomach "tank." Your emotional, spiritual, and mental "tanks" also need tending and filling.

In the Year: Cultivation

At this position on the Wheel of the Year, we exert our greatest effort. The days are long and full of work. The crops have been planted, though most have yet to bear fruit. They require constant tending and cultivation. We must spend time in the fields, watering, weeding, and protecting what we grow from insects. The sun is hot; we spend all day beneath it; it may seem thankless and tiring.

We spent the winter inside, in our seeds. We spend the spring cracking our shells, and now we spend the summer growing outward, towards the light of our potential. We spend this time growing into better versions of ourselves, the versions of ourselves that the world is so desperately in need of.

Just as our ancestors spent all day in the fields, watering and weeding, so too we must metaphorically weed and water our minds with efforts of self-improvement. This means that when we recognize ourselves enacting troublesome patterns of behavior, we must pump the brakes in the moment. This takes patience, and diligence.

The work is not just sweaty, tiring, and unrelenting, it is also hard, frustrating, and often thankless. But when the winter comes, when challenges and difficulties occur, we will have food stores to see us through and the inner resources to weather the storm.

If yin is associated with darkness, then its counterpart yang is associated with light. Darkness is the blackness behind our eyelids that allows us to journey within ourselves. Conversely, the brightness of the sun is the light which draws the eyes upwards and outwards, into the outside world.

In the winter we go within; in the summer we go without. Our focus shifts to the world around us, and what we hope to accomplish in it. Our focus turns from the self to the community, and toward our place woven into our web of relations. The body and the mind are in motion; we are no longer meditating on what it is that must be done, or what we hope to do. We spent all winter focusing on the Self, and the inward, thinking about what we can and should do to better ourselves. At the summer solstice, we turn outwards and ask what we can do for our community.

How can we synergistically weave our efforts to the benefit of all? At the spring equinox we made plans; at the summer solstice, we are enacting them.

In the Lifetime: Ꭺᴅᴜʟᴛʜᴏᴏᴅ

We are at the height of life. We are at our greatest power, like the noon sun, at the apex of our strength. We have yet to reap the full fruit of our life, but we are beginning to taste the summer's sweetness. We are past the awkward, spindly stage of adolescence, and we put down firm roots and broad leaves. Our dreams have been fertilized, and we put our efforts into developing the "fruit" of our labors; though not yet ripe, it grows on our branches.

Adulthood is the time when we take the helm of our destiny, and we decide who we will become and how we will play the hand that life has dealt us. Litha occupies the South position on the Wheel of the Year, the direction of Fire. It is when the flame burns hottest, brightest, and longest, propelling our engine forward. This momentum and energy provides us with a magnificent opportunity to accomplish great things. This is a phase to put down roots, overcome obstacles, and grow towards the sun. It is here that we establish our home, our families, and our livelihoods.

Right Livelihood

This step on the Eightfold Path concerns how one spends one's life: your career, vocation, passion. Specifically, it demands that you direct your life's energy into pursuits that do not harm other living beings. This step's simplest interpreation concerns employment; after all, a job is the place where you dedicate most of your time and energy.

If you are practicing the other seven steps of the Eightfold Path, but disregard this one, then you will spend the majority of your day living contrary to these spiritual ideals. It does not make sense to go on meditative retreats, and then to go to work the next day a diploma mill. It is contrary to a vegetarian's spiritual ideals to work at a factory farm. Though these examples are overly simplistic, they demonstrate the cognitive dissonance between beliefs and acts, which is why this step is so important.

Embracing these ideals means embracing them in all parts of your life, not just cherry-picking when it's convenient. This is especially true in terms of one's career. It is not feasible for most people in the USA to sell all of their belongings and start an organic farm and retreat center in the mountains of Colorado. Thus, we must do the best we can with the options given to us.

If you find yourself in a job where you have to deaden your emotions to get through the day, this is a sign that you are in a place that is draining your spirit. Circumstances may have placed you in a financial situation where you are unable to leave a problematic employment situation. The sutras and the teachings say that we can, if we choose, do our best to turn these situations into teachers, and to understand ourselves and others better, and to deepen our compassion. However, if the option to depart from an employment situation that violates Right Livelihood is presented, it should be taken. If the option to effect change in a troublesome employment situation is presented, it should be taken (that is, if it does not risk stripping you of your financial security).

Though easier said than done, we must direct our

energies into those pursuits we believe will bring the most good to the world—or, at the very least, do no harm. By renouncing harm and promoting peace, in this way we promote these things not only in our own lives, but in the world.

Gaia

Goddess, your thighs stained
with birth-waters of creation,
each amniotic \\ pulse \\
rise and fall of an ocean -
moon heaving on your breast :: waxing transition
midwifed yourself into the world
each extended ((contraction)) an act of devotion
to all children yet to be

awaking
eruption.

Afterbirth.
Mother mountain, so great
Himalayas quake
when you smile.
Mauri wara, so vast
your fingers rough
two continents at once.
Manav flame, heart so hot
your passion turns rock
to liquid fire.

Gaia

Goddess, your thighs stained
with birth-waters of creation,,
each amniotic // pulse //
rise and fall of an ocean - -
moon heaving on your breast :: waxing transition
midwifed yourself into the world
each extended ((contraction)) an act of devotion
to all children yet to be

awaiting
eruption.

Afterbirth.
Mother mountain, so great
Himalayas quake
when you smile.
Mami wata, so vast
your fingers touch
two continents at once.
Nanay flame, heart so hot
your passion turns rock
to liquid fire.

Granny wind, so ancient
your breath says every story ever told.

Your body immutable, indisputable,
forged by nebulous cosmic wombs
and Sirius' seminal spark.
You have borne faces of fire, water, and rock
through ages Cambrian and Cretaceous
the lines of time write themselves in geological verse.

You smile beneath asphalt and neon
your Hadean heart never breached
by pipeline or diamond mine;
only the infant mind of humankind
could think themselves so godly.

So I dance on the skin of unadulterated Earth
remembering my origin:
in the embrace of the oceanic ovary
telling stories with the world's windy tongue,
carrying her seismic fire in my heart.

If Motherhood Were a Greenhouse

When your ribcage blossoms like a magnolia
And you open your throat to the bees of my breast
I grow to encompass you
Tree trunk on chain link

Small-handed, thin neck in the loam
Dandelion-child, root-bound
Growing in a pill-bottle
I give you terra-cotta, a song and my breath

If motherhood were a greenhouse
I would shelter you with ten thousand panes of glass

Sun God

Red-coated is the bull
in the field of summer.
Phoenician figure
on the side of an Irish hill

sun grasped between his yellowed horns
piercing the daylight
spilling his lifeblood
across the fields of barley.

Grazing along
a low stone wall
in a land so green
it hurts the eyes

An old god,
a Mithran memory
rutting with the winter
to mount the spring.

This Druid-friend walks
in pollen and rain

—all things
that consummate the Earth

Calves ripen like apples,
their mother's bellies
growing like moons
the land flushes with heat
and religion.

The Alchemy of Flowers

We build our world from spider's webs.
As road trip dreams wheel in our heads,
we spin our tires on long black roads
beneath Orion's belt at midnight.

The noon of life
the southern fire
ripens all good things
alchemical flicker
pale against the day.

The flame that rests
where your ribs meet
chrysanthemum
opens with the highest sun
and the longest-lit hours.

We are flowers, all
growing in rolling hills
transmuting dirt into color
stillness into song.

InterACTivity

The mandala you see on the next page is waiting to be filled up with color and life.

Assign one color to each of the three "seeds" you planted at Ostara.

Hold these colors in your mind. As the colors are blossoming across the page, imagine that the actions you are taking are causing your "seeds" to burst to life.

Use those colors to fill in the "blossom" of the year that you are cultivating.

As you color in the mandala, think about all of the hard work that you have put in this year towards achieving your goals. This is a kind of meditation. Imagine that each stroke of your pencil, marker, or crayon is another action you are taking to bring your goal to life.

Meditation: Right Livelihood

Midsummer, or the noon of life, is when we are at our adult prime. We are at the age of power; we put forth the most effort to manifest and maintain the lives we have built for ourselves. That said: the financial means through which we maintain our lives is of huge karmic significance.

Find a quiet place where you will not be disturbed. Seat yourself comfortably. Take three deep breaths in through the nose and out through the mouth. Feel your whole body relaxing, from the top of your head, all the way down to the tips of your toes and fingers. Likewise, feel the tension melting from your mind. Breathe deeply again three times, in through the nose and out through the mouth. If any thoughts arise, let them drift like clouds across the sky of your mind. In this gentle space in your mind, consider the following questions. Let the answers arise gently in your mind, as if floating up to the surface from a deep pool.

How do you acquire and use the resources necessary for your life? Do you spend the time at your vocation mindfully and fully present? Do you carry your mindfulness and compassion with you even into the workplace? If not, why not?

In Buddhism, the Infinite Knot has many meanings. Because it has no beginning and no end, it is said to represent samsara, the endless cycle of death and rebirth. It is also said to represent the boundless and infinite wisdom of the Buddha, the mutual interdepentdence of method and wisdom, and the intertwining of wisdom and compassion.

The Celtic Knot is another variety of endless knot.
The Celtic knot is, likewise, a single line with no
beginning and no end. It is represents infinity and
the unity of all of creation. This motif appears on
graves, churches, The Book of Kells, and ancient
megalithic architecture. Some say it also represents
faith, can declare unity between two people, and
may also protect against evil spirits.

*tryadhva-vyavasthitāḥ sarva-buddhāḥ prajñāpāramitām āśrityā-
anuttarāṃ samyaksambodhim abhisambuddhāḥ.*

from: the Heart Sutra

Lammas

Lammas

We have reached the first of the Harvest Holidays. "Lammas" derives its name from the Old English hlāfmæsse. "Hlāf" means "loaf; it literally translates to "Mass of Loaves." The Wheel of the Year rolled past its climax of fire at the Summer Solstice. We begin to gather our resources in a time of plenty. However, this time of plenty is tinged with the looming shadow of winter, for our ancestors began to put stores away to hold them against the time of cold. Even in the warmth of the summer season, the descent into winter (and into the self) begins once more. The sun seems all the brighter during this holiday considering the dark shadow of the lean times ahead.

In the Day: ᴇᴀʀʟʏ ᴀꜰᴛᴇʀɴᴏᴏɴ

The sun passed full noon, and begins to dip (ever so slightly) towards the western horizon. People have been working hard all day, and have started to see the fruits of their efforts. The early afternoon is traditionally a time when people take a break for lunch and rest.

In some countries, especially around the Mediterranean, this time is called a siesta. All of the stores close, everyone leaves work, and they go rest for a few hours. Some might argue that this is done because it's simply too hot to work. While this might be true, there's also a larger cultural schema at work here. Recognizing the need for rest is vital. There's a reason that countries with the concept of siesta, such as Spain and Italy, have longer life expectancies and higher margins of happiness than other Western nations.

This is a reminder that no matter how much progress you've made, it's important to take time to rest. No matter how well-oiled the engine, or how well-raised the horse, if you keep running it without any rest, then eventually it will founder and break down. Remember to give yourself permission to recharge and do nothing every once in a while; this is as important to the work as the work itself.

In the Year: ʀᴇᴀᴘɪɴɢ ᴛʜᴇ ꜰɪʀsᴛ ʜᴀʀᴠᴇsᴛ

Lammas marks the wheat harvest. The heart of this holiday is the goodness of grain and bread. The spirit of the grain harvest was believed to live in the fields of wheat; the harvest rendered the spirit homeless. Thus, the custom of creating "corn dollies" or "corn mothers" ("corn" here referring to wheat) was integral; doing this activity gave the spirit of the corn harvest a home once it had been uprooted. This is a common practice throughout much of northern Europe. Though the specifics of the customs vary, the corn dolly is the center of a celebration, whether it

is paraded through town, at the center of a dance, or doused in water to attract rain.

This is the holiday of ovens and grinding stones, of bread and baking. This is the holiday of wheat; the first loaf of bread baked with the year's first wheat was considered magical. The Anglo-Saxons would take the harvest's first loaf and break it into four pieces, which were then placed into the four corners of the barn. This was said to be a guard against thieves and starvation

Just as our ancestors brought the spirit of the harvest in and celebrated it, so can we. This is a time to stop and appreciate the sweat and effort we have put into our endeavors this year. We begin to think about our end goal. What have we gotten out of this year so far? What lessons have we learned? What has brought us joy? What has improved us as people? There are still two more harvest holidays left in the year, so there is still time for us to decide what we would like to harvest from the metaphorical gardens we have planted. How do we want to use what we have grown, and what do we want to store away for later use? This is the time of sorting, using, and storing.

What is the short list of your harvest this year?
What have you learned from it, and how will you use
it as the year bends towards winter? How will it lend
you sustenance and power in the cold times ahead?
We all have dark times in our lives; Lammas is a time
to take stock of the good things and accomplishments
we have in our lives, things that will tide us over
through the "winters" of our emotional lows.

If you have been working on a project this
year, this would be an excellent phase to think about
the tangible victories and accomplishments you've
achieved. It is important over the life cycle of any
endeavor, whether it is starting a business, learning a
new skill, or starting a family, to celebrate milestones.
There is a reason our ancient ancestors celebrated
the harvests. Otherwise, this would be a time of fear
and drudgery as they frantically put away reserves
to prevent winter starvation. It is important to inject
joy into these times. Celebration not only promotes
joy, but prevents burnout. We can celebrate our
milestones, appreciate our growth, and take stock of
our efforts.

In the Lifetime: ᴍɪᴅᴅʟᴇ ᴀɢᴇ

The frenetic vigor of youth has passed, as has the fire of our physical prime. We are still enjoying the sun of our lives, however, and are beginning to taste the fruits of our life's efforts. By this point in our journey through time, we have built something. The seeds planted earlier in life have begun to bear fruit; we have careers, homes, families, businesses, relationships, and successful projects.

In this time in life, the novelty of the new has given way (at least in part) to the victory that is the creation of the comfortable familiar. You have built a life for yourself; it may not be what you expected when you were younger, but it took a lot of hard work, and it is yours. This is something to celebrate.

RIGHT EFFORT

The harvest season marks the beginning of the descent into the dark. We gather up all of our resources to prepare ourselves for the journey into the darkness of winter.

Likewise, the previous the steps on the Eightfold Path are preparing us to enter into the darkness of the Self. This is where we begin our journey into our minds, to observe their true nature, and to actively promote growth and release trauma.

The first two steps on the Eightfold Path had to do with realizing the true nature of reality, and then resolving to do something with this knowledge. The following three steps had to do with how you behave in the world, and how you treat others. All of these are external-facing realizations and decisions. Looking out into the world, you decide to behave in a better way.

This step means looking inward, and deciding to be better within your own mind.

All of the steps prior to this one are helping us accumulate good, rightful knowledge, patterns, and behavior. Now we must take all we have learned and begin to apply them to our own thoughts.

With Right Speech, you decided to speak from a place of compassion and truth; you must decide now to complete this action within your mind. You turn your attention to your own mind, to notice when angry, hurtful, or self-deprecating thoughts arise.

This is not meant to be an exercise in punishment, where you berate yourself endlessly when you notice a less-than-positive thought. Rather, the goal here is take responsibility for the goings-on in your own mind. It is an opportunity to observe how your thoughts arise, and what form they take. It is a chance to notice patterns within your mind, and to uncover what thought patterns may be rooted in trauma or wounds.

You are not your thoughts. Your thoughts are spontaneous mental weather that arises due to your conditioning, experiences, and trauma. Once you realize the source of a harmful thought pattern, and the nature of the wound from which it arises, you are granted the power to begin to change the way you interact with that wound. You are granted the opportunity to release the thought pattern it has held you in.

Someone who was left in the foster care system as a child may have trouble forming relationships as an adult due to lack of trust. They may think, "I am unlovable" or that "everyone is going to leave me." Or, conversely, they may seek to make themself so impressive and self-sufficient that they will be worthy of the love they never received—and perhaps become unapproachable and standoffish as a result. In either case, they may never have a fulfilling friendship or relationship with this wound coloring their every interaction.

But once they name the source of the pattern, and the source of the wound, they can begin to heal from it.

And over time, the wound loses its power.

This step is about going within to do the shadow work. As the wounds are healing, you are actively cultivating a more peaceful mind. In an enlightened being, the unwholesome thoughts of anger, greed, jealousy, etc. would not arise at all. For the rest of us, when these thoughts arise, they lose their power (if we use these practices). Because when we recognize the conditioning or wounding from which the patterns arise, they no longer control us.

Your thoughts are like clouds drifting across the sky of your mind. In meditation, this concept helps us not get too invested in our own mental dialogue, and to rest in the stillness of the "sky," or the mind beyond our thoughts. In life, it helps us not to be too hard on ourselves when harsh, mean, or dark thoughts arise. They are just clouds on the surface of the mind; they are the result of both our conditioning and our wounding. We have the power, with practice, to cultivate a mind where they do not hold sway—and with years of practice, where they rarely appear at all.

I'll Come Back to You in August

stretch out on the back of August
caught in a sun-beam, cat-lazy
baskets overflowing

with tomatoes and corn

dirt ground into the skin
of my gardening fingers
I sing classic rock ballads
to the beans and the basil:
my offering

we give to each other
water for water
breath for breath
each fruiting a life and a death

reincarnating into each other
our bodies blending
these green vines into my mouth
my sweat into this dirt
my bones into this earth

one of these lifetimes
I'll come back to you in August
when the year is yellow
zucchini blossoms in my hair
to give you my body
and to take your breath.

Crow and the Blue Corn Woman

I'm a crow in a cornfield
defying a sack-and-paper man
because I'm in love
with the blue corn woman
with silk tassels in her hair.

She gives me pollen in her upturned hands
I give her all the wind in my wings
I leave gifts to her tucked in fence posts
bottle caps, stolen earrings, and my living heart.

The breeze is one of her lovers
running their hands through her tassels
making her womb heavy with life.
I witness her as she ripens
loving me, sitting on a scarecrow's head.

I press August
between the two glass plates
of my memory
holding her here.

I will fly home
she will be cut down with the summer.
I'll hold the kernel of her
in my beak
sweet as sugarcane
and replant her in the waxing sun.

A Cup of Tea

A writer's cup of tea
steams on a fading summer's window ledge
mandatory
as every old theater requires a chain-rattling ghost
or every bird traces magnetic North.

August got itself tied up in corn stalks
and September will soon be falling down with the
apples
studding stars in the center
as the wagonload of seasons
turns its wheels again
past equal day, equal night.

But still the breath of rejoicing
runs over the lake
as big as a sea
finding a dynasty
tied up inside me
both the root and the tree
Ireland trying keys, unlocking me, finally.

Another ancestors exhales
their breath fogging glass
revealing secret messages:
within these words;
or in the secrets of birds;
or in a snatch of song heard
under the hill.

I pick up this cup of tea
and dream up the poetry
bardic tongue connecting me
underhill, undersea.

The Blue

Water from the heart of a sapphire
leans forward, pulls back
leans forward, pulls back.
I am the torch in the night,
an overflowing of fire;
a star on the breast of the goddess
whose collarbones span the night sky.

This is how the night chases the dawn
and how the tide follows the moon.
So you shipwreck vessels against me
and I leak my molten heart into the sea.

In the seashell of my mind
you clamor against this shore in the night,
hand against sand and skin.

But an abalone to the ear
will not let you hear the ocean's truth
only the seething of your own blood
and the currents of the heart.

You, the beautiful blue,
the wild line between the day and the night,
the side of a yellow fish that catches the sun,
then recedes.

Whenever I touch the water
there is only heat, and steam, and mist
and a wet creature returning to the waves.

InterACTivity

Lammas is the wheat harvest! It is the holiday of bread and baking, and you'll find three baskets of bread drawn on the next page.

Think about what you have accumulated, accomplished, and "harvested" this year. Think about how your accomplishments (1) have benefited you, (2) how they have benefited your community, and (3) how your "harvest" may yet benefit you in dark times to come.

Think about opportunities and relationships that are ready for "harvesting," or taking to the next level.

Sort your metaphorical harvest thus far into the three baskets:

One is for you, one is for the benefit of your community, and one is to put away for the winter.

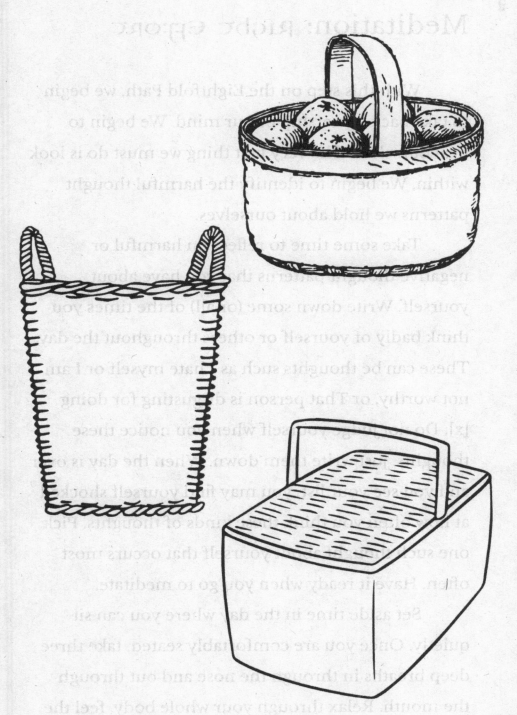

Meditation: Right Effort

With this step on the Eightfold Path, we begin to take back ownership of our mind. We begin to heal ourselves. The very first thing we must do is look within. We begin to identify the harmful thought patterns we hold about ourselves.

Take some time to reflect on harmful or negative thought patterns that you have about yourself. Write down some (or all) of the times you think badly of yourself or others throughout the day. These can be thoughts such as I hate myself or I am not worthy, or That person is disgusting for doing [x]. Do not judge yourself when you notice these thoughts, just write them down. When the day is over and you see your list, you may find yourself shocked at how often you think these kinds of thoughts. Pick one such thought about yourself that occurs most often. Have it ready when you go to meditate.

Set aside time in the day where you can sit quietly. Once you are comfortably seated, take three deep breaths in through the nose and out through the mouth. Relax through your whole body, feel the tension melting away, from the very crown of your head, all the way down to the bottoms of your feet. As the tension leaves your body, feel it also leaving your mind and melting away. Take three more deep breaths. Any thoughts are just drifting clouds; let them be. Rest in this peaceful place for a few moments. Now, gently bring your awareness to a single point between your eyes. At this point, consider the self-harming thought that you brought with you. Do not judge it harshly, do not judge yourself for having this thought. Merely consider it gently. Let it rest in your mind. From deep within you, allow truths to rise up, as if coming to the surface from the bottom of a deep pool. Rest in this process for as long as you need.

When you take the time to notice these thoughts, you can begin to notice patterns among them. Once you notice patterns, you can begin to find the wounds that underlay them. This takes time, so be patient with yourself. Once you identify the wound, you can begin to heal it. Whether you do this on your own, or with the help of a professional, the healing cannot begin until you acknowledge the underlying wound.

The stupa is a Buddhist symbol representing the five elements, which also correspond to various chakras. The base represents Earth, and the root chakra. The rounded portion represents Water, and the sacral chakra. The pillar represents Fire, and the solar plexus chakra. The cap represents Wind, and the throat chakra. Finally, the sun/ moon jewel at the very top represetns Space, and all-encompassing wisdom.

The pentacle is a Pagan symbol that
also represents the five elements.
These elements are Water, Earth, Fire,
Air, and Spirit. It is distinct from the
pentagram in that it is surrounded by
an enclosing circle. The enclosing circle
represents the interconnectivity of all
the elements, and the interrelatedness of
all things.

tasmāj jñātavyam: prajñāpāramitā mahā-mantro mahā-vidyā mantro
'nuttara-mantro samasama-mantraḥ, sarva duḥkha praśamanaḥ,
satyam amithyatāt. prajñāpāramitāyām ukto mantraḥ.

from: the Heart Sutra

maton

Mabon
Autumnal Equinox

The etymology for "Equinox" comes in two parts: from the Latin roots "Aequi," meaning "equal"; and "nox," meaning "night." This is a time of "equal night" and equal day. It is an in-between time where, for the briefest moment, the day and the night are in balance. Night and day each contain the exact same amount of hours. It is a day of little significance to many modern people who do not pay attention to the turning of the seasons. To many, it is simply the end of summer and the start of Pumpkin Spice Season. But what is the equinox, what did it mean to our ancestors, and how is it relevant to us today?

The wheel turns and we spin out our descent into the dark. Our green brethren in the plant nations drop their nuts, fruits, and seeds, to be deposited into the soil to hibernate underneath the winter snow. And then they will grow anew in the spring.

Think about what you have grown this year, and about what you are taking away and tucking away from this year. What kernels of wisdom are you going to take within you as you meditate during the winter's stillness?

In the Day: SUNSET

The sun has moved from late afternoon, and sits on the horizon. We have entered the time of twilight. The bright disc is no longer visible in the sky, but some of its light still lingers.

We've had a busy day. We've accomplished much, and there will always be more we wish had done. We mustn't be too hard on ourselves. We may berate ourselves for all the things we didn't do, but it's important to keep in mind that sometimes simply making it through the day is a monumental feat.

With the sunset, we have the ability to let all of the unaccomplished things go. This is the direction of endings and the closing of cycles. Just as the dawn of the day began with new possibilities, sunset brings with in the closing of possibilities, and ending. We can release into the setting sun all of those things which no longer serve us—all of those angry or unhelpful thought patterns. I wasn't productive enough today. I made a total fool of myself. I behaved in ways I wish I hadn't.

We need to let these things go so that we can get some rest. Our job now is getting enough sleep for the day to come. After all, tomorrow is another day.

In the Year: secoɲd harvest aɲd descent

Mabon, or the Autumnal Equinox, was historically the time for the celebration of the second harvest. This is the time when our ancestors brought in the crops, the literal fruits of their efforts, to strengthen their supplies against the ravages of the bitterest season. Those stores are what sustained them through the dark time. What will sustain you through the winter? What will you hold close to your heart that will keep you warm? What fires will you light within you to shore yourself up against the dark? It is also a time to pause and to reflect the metaphorical "seeds" you planted since the beginning of the year, and the efforts with which you tended them.

The autumnal equinox is the time of the apple harvest. The apple was sacred to the Celts, especially the Irish. No other fruit-bearing tree was hardy enough to grow at such northern latitudes. The apple was a symbol of otherworldly sweetness, a gift of the gods. There was no other tree like it. There is a reason why Bards, the emissaries and mouthpieces of the Divine, are descsribed in the stories as carrying branches of golden apples. If you cut an apple horizontally, the cross-section will reveal a five-pointed star, a pentacle. This fruit is sacred in many ways. It is a useful tool to meditate on the fruits of your own life, and the multiplicity of meanings that can manifest within each accomplishment gained or lesson learned.

Likewise, this equinox is a time to think about what you are reaping, and what you have sowed. Whether you grew an actual garden this year or tackled big, challenging new projects, now is a time to reflect.

This is also a time to give thanks for the bounty all around us. As the crops come in for the harvest, we are surrounded by plenty. We have more than we can eat, more than we need. It is a time for celebration and thanksgiving, and for sharing the fruits of your labor with your community. For what joy is there in growing and creating things if we cannot share them with people who love and care for us? So we think back on those things we have accomplished this year and share them with those around us. With the warmth and comfort of being surrounded by friends, we can take the courage to look at the coming night and the oncoming winter. For although it is a time for feasting and sharing, winter's ascent casts its shadow on this holiday.

From now on, after the Autumnal Equinox, the days will grow shorter, and the nights will grow longer. The darkness gains in power, as well as the cold that comes with it. Just as the Earth and the land descend into the darkness of winter, this is the time in which we prepare to descend into the darkness of your Self. It is a time to shore up your provisions, pack your bag,

and mentally prepare yourself for the road ahead. It is no small undertaking, but ultimately it is necessary in order for us to grow and change as people.

In the Lifetime: Elder years

At this time in our life, we have begun to age. The signs of it are showing on our bodies. Just as the leaves may be starting to turn colors, and the days are getting shorter, our bodies show the evidence of time. We have wrinkles, our bodies don't work quite like they used to, and we find ourselves unable to do many of the things we used to do—or at least, we now have to do them differently.

There's nothing inherently wrong with this. We've reached the time when we can harvest the long work of our lives. Whether we founded a business and have watched it flourish, or started a family and watched the generations grow and thrive, or simply built a web of treasured connections with people we love, we are enjoying the fruits of our years.

However, this is also the time when people begin

to think about death. Just as the leaves fall and the year descends into winter, eventually human bodies fail and return back into the Earth. For many people, death is a thing to fear, and so they put off thinking about it until the very end. However, reckoning with death before the actual event can give life a gravitas and clarity.

After all, if nothing lasts, then this moment is vital and vibrant; it's all we have.

Shadow Work

Shadow Work is many people's least favorite aspect of spiritual growth. The Shadow is all of those aspects of the self that we push down into the depths of ourselves and try to ignore, such as our hurtful behaviors, our traumas, our anger. All is well and good when you are dancing around the Maypole at Beltane, or rejoicing in the high heat of the Summer Solstice. Those times are external, and it is easy to be swept up in the joy of the sun, the light, and community. However, when winter descends, we are left with only

ourselves. And we cannot hide from ourselves forever.

As night overtakes day–culminating in the longest night at the Winter Solstice–we are invited to journey down into our own personal darkness, as the Northern Hemisphere descends into the global darkness of winter.

It is inside our inner darkness that we need the most healing. Yet it is also into those dark places that we shove things down, forget them, and let them fester into anxiety, neuroses, and mental illness. Only by facing them can we ever hope to heal. And it is not easy–it can be compared to what Joseph Campbell called the Long Night of the Soul.

So I challenge you to stand here, on the liminal line between equal day and equal night. Let the sun warm your back, and take bravery from your friends around you as you give thanks and gratitude for all of your blessings. Let them fortify you for the journey to come. And then walk down to face your demons.

Yet, a point worthy of note is that your demons are not angry phantoms whose only twisted joy is haunting you in the night. They are lonely, sad, forgotten aspects of yourself that have not been held, healed, or offered compassion. So as you go downward, into winter and into your Self, remember that one of the greatest things you can do is forgive yourself, and find the courage to change.

Right Mindfullness

As we have striven to learn the lessons of the eightfold path, we round toward the final spokes on the wheel, and toward Right Mindfulness. Mindfulness, to some, means being aware of, and controlling your thoughts—as has been described in the first seven steps of the Path. But more importantly, it means to be fully present in each moment. When you are mindful, you are not casting your mind off into the future with anxiety, into grief about the past, or other far-off daydreams. You are giving your full attention to where you are, right here, right now.

This is the greatest gift you could possibly give to yourself, and to others. The future doesn't exist yet. The past is gone. The present moment is all that is truly real. To allow yourself to fully inhabit it, consciously and mindfully, will give you a degree of immediacy and clarity you've never known.

Similarly, people can tell when you're present, and when you're not. They can tell when "the lights are on, but you've stepped out of the house."

Conversely, they can also feel the intensity of your presence when you fully inhabit the present moment. It is a high gift to receive someone's full presence. Being able to give your full, honest attention to anyone or anything at any moment gives life immediacy, vibrancy, and intensity.

In order to do this, we must cast off our entire society's mindset. Our world constantly seeks to distract us. It wants us worrying about things that have not yet come to pass, mired in the mud of our pasts, or dreaming of far-off, unreal places and things. This is a mindset you must let die; but when you do, you will be putting yourself at odds with your culture. Once you step past this threshold, people will notice you are different, other, immediate, here. For some, it may make it hard to relate to you. You must decide if you are willing to do this. For myself, I can assure you it was the best thing I ever did.

Hebrews 12:29

Equinox again
the trees are lighting themselves on fire
like monks raging against the injustice of winter
raging, raging against the dark

The wind shakes showers of fire down from the forest
each leaf offering itself up for crucifixion
bleeding back down to the Earth
lambasting for one
isolated
moment of nirvana on the way down

The days contract, labor pains that signal
summer hemorrhaging out its life over the autumn
her body lies curled up somewhere under the colored
carpet
Persephone, personified

Each tree
is the burnt-out arm of a galaxy
a pillar of the oncoming night

when the forest of candles flickers out:
stillness, Siddhartha, sanctuary

The sun and Earth dance in equinox and
fear of death spins out religion
Each wooden candelabrum holds a heart pulsing with
belief.

September Girl

She is autumnal
she brings piles of leaves with her everywhere
a trail of rot through doorsteps and fire escapes.

She's got a highway running through her head,
and a way of leaving her heart in foreign countries
with people she's barely met, as the leaves are
changing.

She's chasing some kind of always-oncoming dragon,
never arriving, always missing her bus, she laughs
guffaw, gusto, in a bright and rainy October wind.

She's gardening, going fallow, and decomposing.
A dress made of compost and fingers made of trowels,
digging in for a winter that her soul knows is coming

knowing that she and the winter
must die before anything sprouts.

What was lost

A feeling of vastness
great waters spreading
beneath cold toes,
a connecting pulse
to a bright field of stars
above thin fingers.

As a child I swam through the world
as if it were an ocean filled with phosphorescent fish
its bioluminescence a blazing brushstroke
painted across my heart
surging and receding
thud thud, heart beat
thud thud, heart beat
surge, recede, surge, recede.

I was a jellyfish, permeable,
open, uplifted by water
but life smears seashells across us all
each calcifying pigment
tinted with a moment of grief

colored by loss
darkened by fear.

And so, in dark waters
we cement ourselves to the nearest solid thing
barnacle to humpback
mollusk to rock
a broken heart to someone it does not love
exhaling bubbles
crushed by the pressure
in a million tons of the salty deep.

But in a moment of brilliance
a shaft of sunlight will trace
the long journey down
phytoplankton will ignite fires in their bellies
lighting a watery road back home.
Light may come
on the exhaled breath of a song
a friend's long memory
or a story
that reminds you that you were once brave
slaying leviathans

sailing your ship towards the edge of the world.

Breathe in the heat of a distant star
bloom outwards from this enclosing oyster
and then, little nautilus,
your cocoon will crack to discover
you have grown not one heart, but three
like the octopus, the seabed's flower
you will have one heart for movement
one heart for laughter
and one heart to lead others from the deep.

Autumn Rain

Rain smearing lights down my window
Impressionistic imprints,
Rembrandt smearing color down my spine.
Dappled purple and red
a vivid garden, captured, flattened
like butterfly wings between glass plates.

These rainy evenings remind me
of teenage times
when everything was big and raw
and ramshackle revelations flattened me
preserving my pastel spirits in a jar.

I will not romanticize those years
with young love haze and glory days
but I will remember the rainbows refracted under my
skin
discovering the light of new suns
new pain and new beauty.

With the chuckling rumble of lightning

I remember how my first love laughed
and how I let it drip from between my fingers like
river water
because I was sixteen and what did I know?
But man, how that boy made me glow.

Above blurry street-lamps, the low-hanging clouds
of my memory remember me, so very
thin, like a growing moon
but colored like a dawn.
Rain drips down the glass sides of mind
and my memories dance, weightless.

InterACTivity

The autumnal equinox is the second harvest festival. Apples are harvested at this time. See the tree below? See the apple hanging from its branch? Your accomplishments are like apples.

Write your accomplishments like apples hanging off of the branches.

These words should sprout from the branches, like the apples that are currently being harvested. As you do so, reflect on all of the time and effort you put into achieving your goals. Think about the path that has brought you this far, and your journey through the year. Apples are sweet, but picking them can be hard work; relish the sweetness as well as the challenges of your journey.

Meditation: Rɪɢʜᴛ Mɪɴᴅꜰᴜʟʟɴᴇꜱꜱ

Get outside, if at all possible. Take a break from your normal surroundings. When you spend all of your time in the same place it can become a mental "dead zone." You don't really notice the things around you anymore.

In this outdoor place, whether it's a city street or your driveway, begin the following exercise:

Spot five things that you can see. They can be mundane or beautiful, it doesn't matter. Dwell on each one, not judging it either way, just considering each thing's innate properties and state of being.

Acknowledge four things you can touch. Use your hands to explore the textures of these different objects, and dedicate your attention to this tactile sensory input.

Listen for three things that you can hear. Birdsong, the hum of the refrigerator, the breeze in the trees, all of these are acceptable. Everything has a unique sound; open yourself up to it.

Look for two things you can smell. Most people

aren't used to using their nose in everyday situations. However, the sense of smell is the sense most strongly linked to our sense of memory. What memories awaken with these smells?

Finally, what is one thing that you can taste? Is it the lingering flavor from breakfast? Is there an especially strong flavor on the wind?

This is an exercise used to help people who are experiencing anxiety attacks; however, it can be used by anyone who is trying to cultivate mindfulness, and trying to fully occupy the present moment.

This symbol, called a mitsutomoe, represents the three aspects of Dependent Relationship that give rise to all functioning things. Firstly, things exist due to causes and conditions. Second, phenomena rely on the relationship of a whole to its parts. Finally, phenomena depend upon the disgnation of the mind. The mind is a non-physical thing that cannot be reduced to mere matter. These three teardrops swirl in motion because they represent the impermance and ever-changing nature of all compound phenomena.

This ancient symbol is called the Triskelion, from the Greek word for "three legs." This symbol is inscribed at the entrance of Newgrange, an ancient megalithic whose inner cavern catches the first rays of the summer solstice sun. The number three was sacred to the ancient Celts, and this symbol can represent numerous things, such as: life/ death/rebirth, mother/father/child, past/ present/future, and creation/preservation/ destruction, among others.

tadyathā: gate gate pāragate pārasaṃgate bodhi svāhā.

from: the Heart Sutra

samhain

Samhain

There are two possible interpretations of this name. One says it derives from Old Irish samfuin, meaning "summer's end." Others believe it derives from Proto-Indo-European *sam ("together"). Cognates include Old High German saman, Gothic samana, and Sanskrit samaná, all of which mean "together." This is the time of year that people would come together into their strongholds and groupings to wait out the winter. More metaphorically, it is also the time when the deceased ancestors come together with the living. Samhain signals the death of the year. The final crops have been harvested. The sunlight has continued to wane, and so has warmth. Cold and darkness encroach upon the Earth. The year cycles towards yin energy, or stillness—introspection, and quiet. It is the darkness of the tomb.

It is a time of taking stock. In a literal sense, our

ancient ancestors would take stock of what supplies they had, and compare it to how much they needed to last through the winter. In a metaphorical sense, this is when we take stock of our soul, and find out if we have what we need to be who we truly are (or wish to be).

In the Day: ᴇᴀʀʟy Nɪɢʜᴛ

The sun has completely faded from the horizon. Even the faint lingering twilight has faded. Darkness has enfolded the world; this is the point when the dawn seems farthest away. We have a long night ahead of us.

This is the time for bedding down, and letting our consciousness slip off. We dive from the realm of the conscious into the unconscious. We surrender the waking mind to the world of dreams. Allowing your brain time to turn off lets your body rest and recuperate. If our ancestors were unable to sleep, they gathered around fires and passed the time away—just as today we descend into our kitchens at 3am in dim lighting to drink cups of coffee.

For those who fear the darkness, and what the silence and blackness will bring, this can be a terrifying time; because, after all, in the night the only person we're left with is ourselves.

In the Year: Between Death and Life

The time when Death is manifests is also a time when the borders between the worlds are thinnest, and the dead reach out to us in life. As we take the time to examine our life over the past year, the ancestors offer up to us the stories of their lifetimes. We can see the story of ourselves in the past solar cycle, and we can also see the stories of our ancestors in their past life cycles. We can see our similar joys and failures, our triumphs and our sorrows. In a way, we feel less alone, knowing the stories of those who have gone before. They offer up to us their lessons, that we may learn from their mistakes. They are our teachers, showing us their own darkness, and their own light.

183

When we become introspective and take stock of our year, we will inevitably locate things with which we are not satisfied, things we wish we could do over—do better. There are people we hurt, situations where we disappointed, things we let fall apart. The ancestors teach us how to move into these shadows, and move past them with strength and grace. They show us their own histories of pain and suffering so that we may not feel so alone, and that we may see ourselves reflected in them. But we also see the darkened corners of our psyches, where we need to shine the light, and where we need to change and grow. Admitting to the dark parts of ourselves is painful. The ancestors show us how to do it with their own stories.

In the Lifetime: ᴅᴇᴀᴛʜ ᴀɴᴅ ᴀɴᴄᴇꜱᴛᴏʀꜱ

Samhain is the door to death. In the time between Samhain and Yule, we are in-between realities. It is the darkness that is before life, but after death. In the cycle of reincarnation, it is the period before you incarnate into your next lifetime. In this sense, it is the time when you sit with all of the experiences you learned in your previous lifetime, and reflect upon them. Who you were, how you lived, how much you loved, and your regrets.

If you do not believe in reincarnation, then take the example in the death of a loved one. If their death is represented by Samhain, then in the time after their death, we grieve. We take stock of their life, and our interactions with that person. Did we show them the depth and breadth of our care for them? Or if we withheld affection for some reason or other, do we regret this choice, or not doing so. The period of Samhain can be understood as this period of grieving and re-adjustment. Life as we knew it has come to an end, and we exist in a liminal, in-between state as we figure out how to exist in the world without this person in it.

RIGHT CONCENTRATION

Samhain is tied to the death of the year, and to the death of the human body. Right concentration is intimately linked with the death of the ego. Just as physical death is liberation from the confines of the body, ego death is liberation from the confines of one's mind.

All previous steps on the Eightfold Path have sought to teach you something in regards that you must do. Some effort you must take, some mind frame you must be in, some set of actions you must undertake. Right Concentration has to do with none of these things. There is nothing you must do. You must simply learn to be.

The key to this step on the Eightfold Path is a meditation practice. Meditation is the fundamental core of almost every variety of Buddhism. Why? Because the human mind, and the ego, are very loud and very noisy. Teachers call the thinking part of our brain the "monkey mind." It is constantly chattering about how you couldn't possibly accomplish that thing, that you're too hot or too cold, that there's a pain in your left foot, and what is that woman wearing?

The ego is very attached to the monkey mind; by thinking, it proves its own existence. When you try to stop thinking, the ego fights back very hard, because it very much wants to exist. This leads to the paradox: when someone wants to start meditating, their mind suddenly seems to become much noisier. Then they give up and say that meditation is just something they can't do.

To those people, I say this: when you start meditating, your mind isn't suddenly getting noisier. You're just slowing down enough to finally recognize how noisy your mind is. And that's the point of meditation, to realize that your buzzing thoughts are just noise. And when you realize they're just noise, you can let them go without getting so hung up on them. Eventually, there will be less noise in the first place.

And what happens then, when the mind finally becomes quiet? When the ego is no longer so caught up in proving that it absolutely must exist, you'll experience something profound and transpersonal. What that thing is, more eloquent teachers than I have been attempting to describe for thousands of years. Suffice to say, it will be the death of your previous limited understanding of the world, and liberation from your limited understandings of your Self.

Calling Backwards

Walking backwards down the sidewalks
of my ancestry, the catacombs in my genome.
Beginning where we ended up.

Finally finding the fractions of myself
cast along the steely waters
where the seal-people dwell
Christians told me this was Hell
but it's home.

The green shores of an isle
spun from moss and heather
and raven's feathers;
I've come to the shore again
of the Morrigan
and a herd of white cattle
welcomes my return.
The Christians told me I would burn.

Before, I skipped down childhood cul-de-sacs
unaware of my own attack

as I hop-scotched down a rootless continent.
How I took from others just by being here.

Trying to play with anyone near me
wondering why the spirits couldn't hear me
as I rang out to them in a conqueror's tongue.
I didn't know how long ago this had begun.

Now I sing out in sentences
cut short through lack of knowledge
cut off like sprigs of mistletoe
remembering ways of long ago.

I sing with a spirit
that grasps for the root
of the world.
I call out to my ancestors
with a fractured tongue
but they catch the shards
that refract my heart.

Óró 'Sé do bheatha 'bhaile,
Óró 'Sé do bheatha 'bhaile,
Óró 'Sé do bheatha 'bhaile,
Anois ar theacht an tsamhraidh

To Remember

Long ago
my grandmothers
carried the weight of Europe on their backs
remembering sacred springs.

Ancestors reach down with shriveled fingers
speaking in muffled words
as if through water, faces obscured
by the aquatic skew of time.

A figure with three faces, goddess,
extends the bough of golden apples
in dreamscapes clouded by half-recalled songs.
She says

        Take these sacred words to the people

        Awaken their hearts and their memories

        to the blood and pulse of the Earth.

        Jar them from complacency to reverence

        and to compassion from ignorance

        focail naofa

dúisigh
an domhain croí
urram, trua

The Dreamer doesn't understand.
Her ancestors' tongue was long ago ripped
from her throat
by people who came across the sea.
The sacred melodies forgotten,
ceremonies scattered across three realms.

Invaders ripped the soul
from the chest of the land
put it into a crown and a hand
steeled by a God with no compassion for pagans
and this is why she cannot speak, or listen.

But
she reaches back along her lineage
along the roots of the tree
that binds the world.
Puts her ear to waterways, sensing slow
vibrations

and a heartbeat of stone.
Keeps her ear to the wind,
hitched on to the breath of the sky
and cradles oak saplings,
their heart-fires forged by the sun
Listening for an domhain croi
hearing words like distant thunder.

Tin Horses

A stampede of tin horses
is rolling across the cardboard prairies
tarnished withers beading sweat
they stand like empty oil train cars in the rain.

There is a tin horse for every moment gnawed off by
nostalgia
for every time you've said things were better then.
For all the times your ass met the barstool and
you mixed old regrets with whiskey

There was once something childlike in their soldered
eyes
all now surrendered to apathy and age
of Bronze and Iron, all buried
beneath the soil of centuries.

Tin horses line the hallways in your veins
draped in white sheets to ward off dust
neatly arranged on your inner shelves, the lines of
your ribs
hollow metal ghosts.

Ghost Girl

Under a rain-wet willow tree
this is where the girl I used to be
hides (and died). Ghost of October,
she was always only ever half-alive
never really able to bridge the divide
between my body and the truth;

She is the point from which I jumped
and grew wings; the cicada shell I left behind.
Like a library book kept long overdue
a fictitious telling, only ever half- true
it's what I was told—who I had to be;

So to the ghost-girl in the willow tree;
who felt safe when the kids
played in the cul-de-sac
but got lost as soon as you
got shuffled in with the girls
(or the boys for that matter);

You, will-o-the-wisp, hoping to starve
your way to Woman:

you, thin, hoping that in
the line of your ribs you could finally read
the truth of who you were supposed to be;

Ghost-girl,
I'm giving you your own feathers.
Whoever you are, you don't have
to be me. Fly on, fly on
I'm ready to let you die;

Little ghost, go
to the sky of the spirit world
where we can each be ourselves, our bird selves
shed the weight of skins
we were never meant to inhabit.
Each stroke of our wings a movement that brings
us closer to who we were meant to be

InterACTivity

Asking for the wisdom of those who have come before is wise in and of itself. Think about patterns of behavior you are ready to let go of: codependency, addiction, loneliness, etc. Write them down.

This activity necessitates that you create sacred space in whatever ways you feel called, in accordance with your own tradition or traditions. Bring your list with you.

Get comfortable, and invite your ancestors and your Beloved Dead to come forth. Sit for as long as you need with them. Ask them for their wisdom.

Darken your space. Some find it helpful to gaze at a lit candle to focus. Think of the ancestor you wish to contact, the wise person whose advice you would seek. Hold your focus and ask your question. Keep your mind still as you listen for their response.

199

InterACTivity

Asking for the wisdom of those who have come before is wise in and of itself. Think about patterns of behavior you are ready to let go of: codependency, addiction, loneliness, etc. Write them down.

This activity necessitates that you create sacred space in whatever ways you feel called, in accordance with your own tradition or traditions. Bring your list with you.

Get comfortable, and invite your ancestors and your Beloved Dead to come forth. Sit for as long as you need with them. Ask them for their wisdom.

Darken your space. Some find it helpful to gaze at a lit candle to focus. Think of the ancestor you wish to contact, the wise person whose advice you would seek. Hold your focus and ask your question. Keep your mind still as you listen for their response.

If you are unable to think of a specific ancestor, that's ok. Hold your focus and ask for an ancestor to come forward. Hold your focus, ask your question in your mind, and keep your mind still as you listen for their response.

Once you have heard their answers, thank them for their insight. Then, send them on their way.

Go forward humbly and with love. Now is the best time to ask for their wisdom, because the veil between the worlds is thinnest. Put forward your questions to them. Then, listen to their guidance about how to make these changes and carry forward in your life.

Write their advice for you on the next page.

If you are unable to think of a specific ancestor,
that's ok. Hold your focus and ask for an ancestor to
come forward. Hold your focus, ask your question in
your mind and keep your mind still as you listen for
their response.

Once you have heard their answers, thank
them for their insight. Then, send them on their
way.

Go forward humbly and with love. Now is the
best time to ask for their wisdom, because the veil
between the worlds is thinnest. Put forward your
questions to them. Then, listen to their guidance
about how to make these changes and carry forward
in your life.

Write their advice for you on
the next page.

Meditation: Right Concentration

Give yourself a sizable chunk of time to sit in your quiet place. Find your comfortable seat and settle in. As always, take three good, deep breaths in through the nose and out through the mouth.

Begin to relax your whole body. Feel ease flowing slowly and gently from the top of your head down the length of your neck, torso, arms, and legs. Relax your jaw. Feel it all flow out, all the way to the tips of your fingers and toes. Feel your muscles be loose and at ease.

Now let the tension leave your mind. Breathe deeply three times, in through the nose and out through the mouth. Begin to let your thoughts drift like clouds. Just passing visitors in the sky of your mind. Breathe deeply and let them go.

Gently bring your awareness to the point between your eyes. Let your awareness rest here. Continue to let your thoughts gently drift. Sit in your awareness. If you notice your mind wandering, carefully return it to the point between your eyes.

Attend this process with forgiveness and humor; you are just beginning. Stay here in this calm place for as long as you are able.

Meditation is a process, and a skill. And just like any skill, it is challenging at the start. You may notice your mind wandering often. Excellent! This are great opportunities to practice forgiveness and humor with the process, and to cultivate compassion with yourself. You do not need to be "good" at it, you merely need to do it. Each difficulty has the opportunity to be an excellent teacher—just never fall into the trap of taking yourself or this process too seriously. In this way, you can befriend your mind.

The eyes of the Buddha represent the all-seeing wisdom, knowledge, and compassion of the Buddha. The wisdom and true nature of the Buddha resides within all things and within all people. The swirl between the Buddha's eyes represents the character meaning "one," or the perfect unity when one reaches Nirvana.

The goddess figure represents the Eternal Mother archetype. She births and nurtures all beings. She is the Mother of All; all descend from her, and when we die, all will return to her. The swirl within the goddess figure represents the generative power of the Divine Feminine and the ability to bring forth new life.

iti prajñāpāramitā-hṛdayam samāptam

from: the Heart Sutra

YULE

Yule

The word "Yule" is descended from the Old Norse jōl, the name of the ancestral winter feast lasting 12 days, the name of which was later appropriated for Christmas. If Samhain is the darkness of the tomb, then Yule is the darkness of the womb. With this understanding of Samhain, Yule takes on a rich array of symbolic meanings. One of these is the incarnation of the human soul into new life. Another is the moment that we figure out a way to pick up the pieces, readjust, and continue forward after someone we love has died; it is, fundamentally, a new lifetime. The world is a different one than it was before. It is the start of a new cycle, because the old cycle has ended.

The time between Samhain and Yule is the time in which we allow ourselves to grieve. It is the time in which we allow ourselves to process our year, our triumphs, our failures, and our Selves. We are at our deepest point, and all can seem lost—until we go within, and start to sort what we find there.

In the Day: ᴍᴉᴆᴎᴉᴦʜᴛ

We have rounded the longest part of the night, and now we ascend towards the dawn. Most of us are still fast asleep, deep in the world of the unconscious mind. Our minds are resting and our bodies are recuperating. Our minds are filtering and processing the events of the day in rapid-fire and oftentimes nonsensical dreams.

This darkest part of night is representative of the deepest part of the human subconscious, the part that is farthest from our conscious knowing, just as midnight is farthest from the full height of the noon sun. Darkness is at its full power. This time is called "the witching hour" for a reason. The subconscious mind knows that in order to ritually or ceremonially separate the Self from ordinary reality, entering the darkness is often vital. We must descend into the darkness of the Self as we descend into the darkness of the night.

In the Year: ANCESTRAL PRACTICES AND BELIEFS

Christians have designated Yule as the time of the birth of their messiah, perhaps because of the connotations of the womb and birth. While this holiday can be associated strongly with the yin aspect, it is also located in the North of the Wheel of the Year, associated with the element of Earth and the stillness of stone--opposite to the blazing fire, heat, action, and movement of Summer Solstice located at the south of the Wheel.

The darkness of winter is the darkness of the womb, and Yule is the day of rebirth. It is pertinent to mention Mōdraniht (Old English "Night of the Mothers" or "Mothers' Night"). This holiday was observed sometime around Christmas Eve, and involved ceremonies and devotions to several triple goddesses. While details surrounding it are sparse, it is perhaps related to the Norse dísablót. It is unsurprising that mothers were venerated at this time, and asked to take part in ceremonies to birth the New Year into being.

To this day, the reindeer is strongly associated with Yule. While the male reindeer lose their antlers in the winter, the females do not. It is elder female reindeer, not males, that lead the herd. While the sun (the active yang element) declines with the waning year, the nurturing element (reindeer, and yin), grows in strength. Most nowadays associate reindeer with Santa Claus, but in ancestral times the female reindeer was sacred.

This includes Saule, the Latvian and Lithuanian sun goddess, whose sleigh is pulled by female reindeer; Rohanitsa, who is often depicted with antlers, and who births children in both human- and deer-shape; and the reindeer of the circumpolar peoples of Scandinavia and Siberia whose urine assists the predominantly-female shamans in the process of entheogenic journeys aided by the Amanita muscaria mushroom. Reindeer were common in Ireland, Scotland and Britain many thousand years ago, though with recession of the ice age they disappeared from the isles. Despite disappearing from the isles, there is evidence that a deer goddess cult persisted in the north of the Isles for thousands of years.

The Deer Mother is a well-known mythological archetype throughout the world. As a prey animal, it is likely that she was one of the first spirit-beings to be venerated by humankind as a source of food and materials for clothing and tools. Deer Mother gives of herself that the people may have life; this is the archetype of the Mother, who gives of their body to nurture their children physically in the womb and while nursing.

This nurturing archetype, coupled with yin energy, exemplifies the energy of the holiday. The nurturing stillness of the womb gives birth to the new sun and the beginning of a new cycle. Then, like a newborn babe, it shelters and protects us as the year slowly waxes, embodying the cycle of infancy into childhood.

Deer Mother sacrificed—and continues to

sacrifice—herself so that her children may live. This is why, at this time, we honor her by going into the meditative stillness that exists within all of us, and allowing ourselves to rest.

In the Lifetime: ℕEᘺᗷORℕ

The sun is reborn. The days will lengthen. The Longest Night has ended. We have survived. This is the feeling of the sunrise on Solstice morning. The waxing and the rebirth. It is the newborn year emerging from the womb of death, the Sun God returning after his long decline.

At Samhain a part of us died—the parts that no longer served us; the destructive patterns of behavior; the limiting systems of belief. We mourned these things in the descent into the longest night, pondering who we might become. And after we have walked the labyrinth all the way inwards, we find ourselves at the center of possibility, an egg that is on the cusp of hatching.

This holiday is associated with the stillness and silence of yin, the receptive aspect. It is the direct opposite of the summer solstice, yang-energy—a time for external activity, celebration, community, and interaction. Yin is associated with the creative and nurturing womb-space, which is central to the rebirth-aspect of this holiday.

This is the time when we revel in the very miracle of being alive. This is the time when the icy wind and the blowing snow cannot dominate the human spirit. We revel in the fact that we are, that we exist, and that we have survived. We rejoice with our community and tell each other stories to keep the cold at bay.

This holiday is about the resilience of the human spirit. It is about the rebirth of hope. And it is about growing courage within your heart to hold strong until the spring returns.

Right Understanding

The Eightfold Path begins here; at the (re)birth of the sun, we place the first step on the path—at the birth of understanding. Understanding something means to look into it and perceive its truth, to know it. It is the ability to see a thing as it is, without any illusions or opinions about it. It is naked, raw, and honest.

All that forms will dissolve; all that comes together will drift apart; all that is born into light will die into darkness. Impermanence is the true nature of all things—the only constant is change. If all things that rise will fall, then what is the use to clinging to unimportant things? None of us will make it out of life alive. Impermanence necessitates compassion; the other option is a life clouded by fear and anger—for our brief moment in the daylight, we will spend not one minute of it looking at the sun.

Many things block our ability to be compassionate. Mostly, it is our mind. To see reality as it is, we have to realize that our view of reality is clouded by our opinions, our ideas, and our story. We have lived a life that has conditioned us to think in certain ways, to perceive certain things as "good" and "bad," as "beautiful" and "ugly." And because everyone has a different mind that has been shaped by a different life, their perceptions about the meanings of these things vary infinitely. Where, then, is the truth?

The truth is that a rock is not good or bad. A duck is not ugly or beautiful. These are constructs of the human mind. The rock will continue to sit in a field; the duck will continue to swim regardless of our opinion about it. Our perceptions live in our minds, not out in the world. We judge a thing to be a certain way—smart or stupid, fast or slow—and then the judgement settles in our mind. But the judgement lives in the mind, not in the world. Accepting this is the first step on the eightfold path, to Understanding.

Once we accept this fundamental truth about reality, we become free.

Yule

When the sun rises on solstice
I call gratitude to Mother Reindeer
who placed her heart at the center of creation
that the world may have life.

When the Yuletide sun dances the line
of the eastern horizon
for the briefest moment,
for the span of a flashing star
we spread our arms in thanks,
gathering the people about our fire
that we may tell them a story.

When I wake in the morning
to the breathing of someone I love
in the twilit gray of winter's day,
the warmth in my heart radiates
in the laundry pile, in the curtains, and the doorknob;
I count the blessings lined up on the dresser,
and along the walls.

Stirring myself from dreams that echo my ancestors,
walking barefoot on the gravel road before me
the Good Road;
carrying the Way forward, out of sleep
and into the Dream we all dream together
(that is the world).

And though the sun rises but briefly,
I find a solace
that buds with my inner spring,
an appreciation of the challenges
that have tested me so sorely.

The spirits walk towards us from all four directions
above, below, and center
and gather around our fire
as we tell their stories through the longest night.

Threshold of Night

We have crossed the threshold of night
held death's face sweetly
and curled up in our hillside tombs
which weather warps to snowy wombs.

Breath fogging on solstice morning
a virgin sun spills upward
rising for the first day in a lifetime.

Ice, stillness, and blue sky
the creeping cold
caribou crossing the horizon.

Blessed, or cursed, with a second birth
the weight of centuries and cycles
ours now left to lift, or live.

Heart of Darkness

Curse the noisy stars
the trumpeting moon
the snow shouts light from underfoot.
The ice fills all my senses
with an electric overflowing
unasked-for brilliance.

I turn off the lights
inside my body;
cap the candles
in my mind.

Wrapped in the blanket of night
sequestered by the embers
a blizzard yowls
outside the house of my skin.

I lay in the slow flow
of my nest of blood
in the careful dance of light

across my nerves:
a regulated universe,
heart-measured.

Recluse inside my body
beyond the reach of winter's hound
and the pounding waves of snow
embryonic, I rest
in the heart of darkness.

She Merely Sleeps

Ice-sky void of birds
finger-trees free of song
stream locked up with glass
witness the song of a desolate heart
unwise to the slow pulse of the world.

The caribou knows her
the white fox sees her
the sky-lights dancing
to the strains of the heavenly spheres
waiver to her long drumbeat.

Spirits concave like rib bones
we shore up stores for the long cold
to keep the hunger pains at bay
but not to beat back the starvation of the heart.
That is the work of grandmothers.

Who weave stories
onto the loom of the North Star
joining the threads of legends
through the warp and weft of winter.

Knowing she merely sleeps,
the goddess,
in the mantle of ice
snowdrops pulsing in her dreaming eyes.

Yule is the season when we snuggle in, like
the seeds snuggled into the soil awaiting the spring.
Just as the seed is hidden beneath the ground, so
too hidden aspects of ourselves live beneath our
conscious mind.

Trace the labyrinth on the next
page.

At several points there will be a
symbol with a page number.

Follow the page number to
the marked line of the poem that
matches it earlier in the book.

As you journey inward into the labyrinth,
imagine yourself going further and further inward
into your Self. Allow yourself to be open to what you
may find there.

InterACTivity

Yule is the season when we snuggle in, like the seeds snuggled into the soil awaiting the spring. Just as the seed is hidden beneath the ground, so too hidden aspects of ourselves live beneath our conscious mind.

Trace the labyrinth on the next page.

At several points there will be a symbol with a page number.

Follow the page number to the marked line of the poem that matches it earlier in the book.

As you journey inward into the labyrinth, imagine yourself going further and further inward into your Self. Allow yourself to be open to what you may find there.

A new poem will be constructed out of the lines you discover as you journey inward into the labyrinth.

232

InterACTivity

As you pass each number on the labyrinth, write each line on the next page to form the hidden new poem and message.

1 - page 32 - Line 2

2 - page 55 - Line 9

3 - page 82 - Line 9

4 - page 108 - Line 6

5 - page 136 - Line 14

6 - page 169 - Line 5

7 - page 195 - Line 5

8 - page 222 - Line 7

Meditation: RIGHT UNDERSTANDING

One simple truth is that nothing lasts forever. This is the nature of impermanence. Everything fades to dust. If this is so, why do we cling to things, to our own detriment? The only constant is change. Yet we put our energy into, and prioritize things that, at the end of our lives, will seem very trivial indeed. Many people covet riches and an extravagant life (though this is distinct from simply desiring enough resources to survive). If all things pass, then all we really have is ourselves and each other, the personality and attitudes we cultivate, and the relationships we invest in.

Go to a quiet place. Comfortably seat yourself. Breathe deeply three times, in through the nose and out through the mouth. Begin the body relaxation process: from the top of the head, gently cascading down to the tips of your fingers and toes. Relaxing the neck and shoulders, unclenching the jaw, and letting your arms and legs hang free and loose. Feel the tension go out of your mind as you breathe deeply. In through the nose, out through the mouth. Release your grip on your thoughts and let them begin to drift. Let them be free. Let your mind be free. Rest here for a moment in this peaceful place.

Now, bring your awareness gently to the point between your eyes. Rest here for a few moments. Breathe in deeply in through the nose and out through the mouth. If your attention wanders, bring it carefully back to the point between your eyes. Now, in this place, allow awareness of impermanence to percolate through your consciousness. The nature of flux, change, life, death, and rebirth. Sit with this awareness, returning to focus when your mind wanders.

After meditating on impermanence, spend some time considering how this knowledge can beneficially affect the "big picture" things in your life: your relationships, your career, your spirituality. How will you spend your time, knowing that it is a finite resource? And how will you treat others, knowing that their time here is as short as yours?

The prayer wheel, also the namesake of this book, is a Buddhist (specifically, Tibetan Buddhist) tool with a mantra (typically om mani padme hum) inscribed on the outside. In the middle is a "Life Tree" with many more mantras inscribed. Spinning the prayer wheel is an act of devotion in motion akin to reciting the mantra. If done rhythmically, it may also aid in inducing a trance state of meditation.

The labyrinth is a Celtic maze. It is a tool
for introspection and meditation through
movement. As one walks the labyrinth, they
go deeper into the maze, and deeper into the
self. It too is a tool for inducing trance. Just
as the prayer wheel holds secret knowledge
within the center, so too do we. By walking
the labyrinth we gain access to this inner
wisdom through motion, just as we do with
the prayer wheel.

THANK

~ supporters ~

This book took a village to make. First, the
artists, many of whom created original art pieces
specifically for this book, without expectation of
being paid. Second, the Illinois Arts Council, who
awarded me the IAS grant that allowed me to
actually pay my artists. Third, to the people whose
monetary contributions to the original GoFundMe
back in 2017 made it possible to kickstart this
process—a special shoutout to one wild woman
lovingly tending a patch of forest in Missouri.
Fourth, the friends (many of whom were among the
original GoFundMe backers) who cheered me on the
whole way. Of course, there is the family that raised
me to suffer no fools and not take no for an answer.
And finally, to my doting Jaybird who has never, not
once, stopped believing in me.

YOU

~ARTISTS~

Cover Art: *Simon Jay Cervania*

Introduction: *Colleen Koziara*

Imbolc: *Ray Espiritu*

Ostara: *Maggie B. Karlin*

Beltane: *Bubba Geisha*

Litha: *Ryan Blume*

Lammas: *Gabriella Mejia*

Mabon: *Ruben Calderon*

Samhain: *Allegra Willow Larson*

Yule: *Allegra Willow Larson*

Mandala: *Amy Hassan*

Labyrinth: *Abby Denlinger*

CPSIA information can be obtained
at www.ICGtesting.com
Printed in the USA
BVHW071328261022
650289BV00006B/18

9 781087 876191